©1999 Robert Frederick Limited
4-5 North Parade
Bath
BA1 1LF

Printed in India

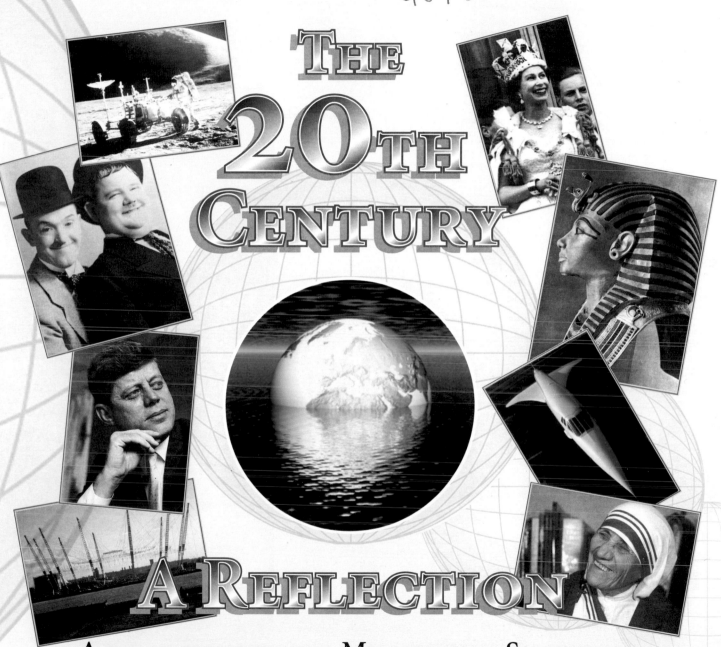

THE 20TH CENTURY

A REFLECTION

**A FULLY ILLUSTRATED MILLENNIUM SOUVENIR
SHOWING IMPORTANT EVENTS AND DATES THROUGHOUT
THE 20TH CENTURY**

1900

Below:
At the turn of the century even educated women had few rights. Their first challenge was to secure the right to vote in elections.

Right:
The South African (Boer) War was a war of imperial supremacy between the British and the Afrikaners -Dutch settlers. It aroused the first significant outpouring of anti-imperialist feeling in Britain. There was rejoicing in the streets when it was finally over in 1902.

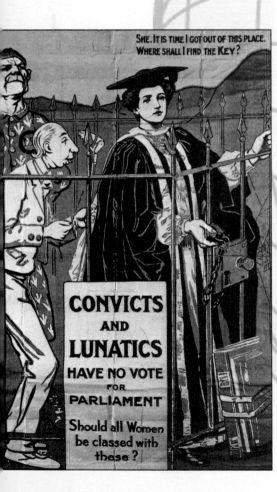

World Events of 1900
- The Paris International Exhibition opens.
- In South Africa the 7 month siege of Mafeking is ended.
- World powers unite against China following the Boxer uprising.
- Coca Cola arrives in Britain.
- Dr Landsteiner discovers 3 different blood groups.
- The Italian King is shot dead by an anarchist.
- The Zeppelin airship makes its first flight.
- The Metro opens in Paris.
- Millions are starving in Indian famine.
- The trade unions create the Labour Representation Committee under its secretary James Ramsey MacDonald.
- The US Senate ratifies the 1899 decree creating an international court of arbitration at The Hague.

Sporting Life
- Ambush II, owned by the Prince of Wales, wins the Grand National.
- Women are allowed to compete in the 2nd Olympic Games. The USA dominates the track and field winning 14 gold medals.
- Automobile enthusiasts compete in a 1,000 mile trial around Britain.
- The Davis Cup tennis tournament is created.

The Arts
- Puccini's "Tosca" is premiered at Covent Garden.
- Oscar Wilde dies in Paris.
- The first films with sound are made.
- The Hippodrome Theatre opens in London's Charing Cross Road.
- "I'm only a bird in a gilded cage" is a hit song.

1901

World Events of 1901
- Queen Victoria dies. She reigned for 64 years.
- J. Pierpont Morgan pulls off the first billion dollar business deal giving him a virtual monopoly of the steel industry.
- Students and workers riot in Russia.
- A total eclipse of the sun is photographed in Mauritius.
- Henri Becquerel discovers that salts of the metal uranium emit rays.
- The company Cadillac is founded in Detroit.
- The first British submarine is launched amid doubts as to its usefulness.
- President McKinley is shot and killed. Roosevelt is sworn in.
- The Eastman Kodak Company is born.
- The first Nobel Prizes are awarded in Sweden.
- London gets a telephone system.
- The first hearing aid is demonstrated.

Sporting Life
- American Robert Walthour breaks the 1 mile cycling record with a time of 1 min. 37.4 secs.
- H Fournier wins the Paris to Berlin automobile race.
- Non-league Tottenham Hotspur win the FA cup.

The Arts
- Rodin shocks the art world with his sculpture of Victor Hugo.
- An exhibition is staged in Paris by a 19 year old Picasso.
- Punch cartoonist Sir John Tenniel retires after 50 years in the job.
- Toulouse-Lautrec dies aged 36.

Below left:
Queen Victoria in 1897 with her great-grandson, who became King Edward VIII.

Below:
The first British submarine.

1902

World Events of 1902
- Britain sees the worst smallpox epidemic in medical history.
- A state of emergency is declared in Ireland.
- Colonial statesman Cecil Rhodes dies.
- The Boer War is ended.
- A law is passed in the US to protect the buffalo.
- In Egypt the Aswan dam is completed.
- Lord Tennyson, son of the poet, is appointed Governor-General of Australia.
- The Nobel Prize for medicine is won by Major Ronald Ross for his discovery of the cause of malaria.
- The 322 ft high Campanile of St Mark's Cathedral in Venice collapses during a safety inspection.
- Edward VII is crowned amid concern for his health.
- St Pierre, capital of Martinique is wiped out by a volcano. One man survives.

Sporting Life
- Ard Patrick wins the Derby.
- Hugh Doherty wins the men's singles final at Wimbledon.
- 20 die as a stand collapses at an England v. Scotland football match in Glasgow.

The Arts
- Sarah Bernhardt returns to the London stage at the age of 58.
- France is shocked by the tragic death of Emil Zola.
- 'The Tale of Peter Rabbit' by Beatrix Potter and 'Just So Stories' by Rudyard Kipling are published.
- Sir Henry Irving stars in Will's Faust.

1903

World Events for 1903

- Speed limits are imposed on roads in Britain, but proposals for driving tests, vehicle inspections or penalties for drink-driving are rejected.
- Atrocities in the Balkans horrify the world.
- Edward VII visits Paris to improve Anglo-French relations.
- The trade name "Pepsi Cola" is registered.
- Popular Pope Leo XIII dies aged 93.
- The Women's Social and Political Union, led by Emmeline Pankhurst, is formed.
- Marie Curie shares the Nobel Physics prize with her husband Pierre and Henri Becquerel for their work on radio-activity.

Sporting Life

- The first Tour de France is won by Maurice Garin. Only 20 out of 60 entrants finished the race.
- England footballer R. E. 'Tip' Foster scored a record 287 runs in test cricket against Australia.

The Arts

- A musical version of "The Wizard of Oz" opens in Broadway.
- The American painter Whistler dies.
- The first western movie, "Kit Carson" opens in the US.
- "Sweet Adeline" is a hit song.
- The late Samuel Butler's novel "The Way of All Flesh" exposes the oppressions of Victorian family life.

1904

World Events for 1904

- Britain and France sign the Entente Cordiale.
- Henry Ford sets a new land speed record of 91.37 mph.
- The new Pope imposes a dress code for women visiting the Vatican.
- The Japanese cripple the Russian Fleet at Port Arthur.
- A continental craze for sending postcards catches on in Britain.
- The Trans-Siberian railway is completed.
- A woman is arrested for smoking on New York's Fifth Avenue.
- The US army believes the Wright's flying machine has no military value.
- Valves will replace the unreliable crystal and cat's-whisker combination in radios.
- The New York subway opens.
- Two trawlers from Hull are sunk by ships of the Russian Baltic Fleet.

Sporting Life

- Manchester City beats Bolton Wanderers 1-0 to win the FA Cup.
- James Jeffries remains the world heavyweight boxing champion.
- The USA again dominates the Olympic Games.

The Arts

- Caruso makes his first recording in the US - "La Donna e Mobile".
- There are exhibitions of paintings by Matisse and Monet in Paris.
- Paris sees the first performance of "Sheherazade" by Ravel.
- The Russian author Chekhov dies.
- "Peter Pan" opens in London.

1905

World Events of 1905
- In St Petersburg 500 strikers loyal to the Czar are gunned down, an event which soon becomes known as "Bloody Sunday".
- Albert Einstein proposes his "Theory of Relativity".
- Dr Barnardo, who founded over 112 children's homes, dies.
- The Wright brothers make their longest flight yet of 38 mins. 3 secs.
- Aspirin is licensed for sale in Britain.
- Motor car accident victims get an ambulance service in London.
- The Norwegian explorer Amundsen finds the magnetic North Pole.
- The first suffragettes go to prison for assaulting the police.
- A peace treaty ends the war between Japan and Russia.

Sporting Life
- The New York Yacht Club in "Atlantic" win a transatlantic race for the German Kaiser's Cup.
- Australian B. B. Kieran swims half a mile in a record 11 mins 28 secs.
- 17 year old May Sutton becomes the first American to win the Wimbledon Ladies Singles title.

The Arts
- Shaw's "Man and Superman" opens at London's Court Theatre.
- Sir Henry Irving dies.
- Sir Arthur Conan Doyle revives his hero Sherlock Holmes.
- Author of "Around the World in 80 Days" Jules Verne, who never travelled, dies in his home town of Amiens.

Below:
A London street market in 1904.

Right:
Italian Operatic tenor Enrico Caruso was one of the first opera singers to achieve fame through gramophone recordings.

1906

World Events of 1906
- The British Empire occupies one fifth of the land surface of the earth.
- The world's biggest and fastest battleship, "HMS Dreadnought" is launched.
- Mount Vesuvius erupts.
- An earthquake devastates San Francisco.
- In France scientists immunise cattle against tuberculosis.
- Edward VII visits his nephew in Germany, the Kaiser Wilhelm II.
- Kidney transplants are performed on cats and dogs in Canada.
- British officers consult with their German counterparts as they plan to modernise the army.
- More suffragettes go to prison.
- Dr Gowland Hopkins suggests there is a link between nutritional deficiencies and serious diseases.

Sporting Life
- Dr Dudley Sargent of Harvard advises women not to take part in rough sports like netball, hockey and lacrosse.
- An interim Olympic Games is held in Athens.
- Hungarian Ferenc Szisz wins the first Le Mans circuit race in a Renault.
- Cambridge beat Harvard in an international university boat race.

The Arts
- The pianist Artur Rubinstein makes his debut in New York.
- The Norwegian playwright Ibsen dies.
- Actress Ellen Terry celebrates 50 years on the London stage.
- "Waiting at the church" is the year's hit song.
- John Galsworthy's "A Man of Property" is published.

1907

World Events of 1907
- The new Criminal Courts of Justice at Old Bailey are opened.
- Plans for a Channel tunnel are abandoned because of the threat to Britain's defences.
- Wine growers riot in France.
- Gandhi declares a campaign of civil disobedience in South Africa.
- In Canada 730 people are rescued from the shipwrecked "Mount Temple".
- The German Kaiser and Kaiserin make a state visit to Britain.
- Baden Powell holds the first "Boy Scouts" camp.
- Dr Herbert Tidswell warns that the dangers of smoking include cancer.
- Paul Cornu, a French bicycle maker shows off his first helicopter.
- Cunard's "Lusitania" breaks the transatlantic record, crossing in 4 days, 19 hours and 52 minutes.

1908

- The world's laziest man, James Thompson of Clare in Ulster, gets out of bed after 29 years.

Sporting Life
- Orby wins the Derby.
- England beats France 41-13 at Rugby.
- Italian Prince Borghese wins the Peking to Paris motor car race.

The Arts
- "The Follies of 1907" is the first revue staged by Florenz Ziegfeld.
- Puccini's "Madame Butterfly" is first performed in English.
- The Metropolitan Opera House bans Richard Strauss's "Salome" calling it 'obscene'.
- "Les Demoiselles d'Avignon" by Picasso causes a sensation.
- Rudyard Kipling wins the Nobel Prize for Literature.

Far left:
HMS Dreadnought was the first of a type that dominated naval warfare until the 1950's. These battleships were replaced by aircraft carriers and more sophisticated submarines.

Right:
In 1908 Dr. W. G. Grace retired from first class cricket after nearly fifty years in the game.

Left:
Elections are won or lost on plans to extend the scope of taxation. Posters like this were the forerunner to modern day party political broadcasts.

World Events of 1908
- 50 year old suffragette leader Emmeline Pankhurst describes life in Holloway prison.
- The King and Crown Prince of Portugal are assassinated.
- The British government introduces the Old Age Pension.
- The "White City" in West London is built to celebrate the Entente Cordiale and host the Olympic Games.
- Edward VII visits the Czar in Russia amid criticism from Labour MPs.
- Henry Ford produces the "Model T" in Detroit.
- Germany shows no interest in attending disarmament talks in The Hague.
- British Prime Minister Asquith announces emergency plans to reduce unemployment.

Sporting Life
- England beats Australia by one wicket in the Test Match.
- 100-1 outsider Signorinetta wins the Derby.
- Great Britain dominates boxing and rowing in the London Olympic Games.
- Jack Johnson becomes the first black boxer to win the world heavyweight championship.

The Arts
- J. J. Duveen makes a gift of a new wing to the Tate Gallery in London.
- James Barrie's play "What Every Woman Knows" is premiered in London.
- "Shine On Harvest Moon" is a hit.
- Elgar's first symphony is performed in Manchester.

1909

Left:
Women campaigning for the right to vote became increasingly militant and some were arrested and imprisoned. Many men supported their cause.

Right:
Controversy has surrounded claims of rival explorers in the quest to reach the North Pole. Cook announced that he had reached the Pole in 1908, but this was later generally dismissed. A study was published in 1989 acknowledging Robert Peary (pictured) to have been the first to conquer the Pole in 1909.

- Lloyd George calls the House of Lords "500 men chosen accidentally from the unemployed".

Sporting Life
- The King's horse Minoru wins the Derby.
- At 41 Arthur Gore becomes the oldest man to win the Wimbledon championships.

The Arts
- Nijinsky stars in the first performance of Diaghilev's Ballets Russes.
- "Anne of Green Gables" by Miss L M Montgomery is published.
- The Victoria and Albert Museum is opened.
- "I wonder who's kissing her now" is a hit.

World Events for 1909
- Europe's worst earthquake in southern Italy claims over 200,000 lives.
- Sales of alcohol are being banned in many states and counties in the USA.
- Count Zeppelin crashes his airship after flying it for a record 37 hours.
- Marconi wins the Nobel Prize for the wireless.
- American shopping in the form of Selfridges comes to London.

- Commander Robert E Peary reaches the North Pole. Frederick E Cook's claim to have reached it before him is dismissed.
- Frenchman Louis Bleriot flies a plane across the Channel.
- Suffragettes refusing food in prison are being force-fed.
- The World's Fair opens in Seattle.
- The USA now has more than 2 million shareholders.

1910

World Events of 1910

- Great Britain mourns the death of Edward VII.
- Halley's comet appears.
- In Paris, floods threaten priceless works of art.
- Mount Etna erupts in Italy.
- Dr Crippen is arrested on a ship bound for Canada for the murder of his wife.
- Kissing is banned on French railways because it delays trains.
- Thousands pack St Paul's Cathedral and line the streets to pay their respects to Florence Nightingale who dies aged 90.
- Japan formally annexes Korea.
- A London doctor says that if lunacy increases at the present rate the insane will outnumber the sane in 40 years.
- A second general election in a year results in a dead heat for the Liberals and Tories.

Sporting Life

- Newcastle United beat Barnsley 2-0 in the FA Cup Final replay at Crystal Palace.
- Lemberg wins the Derby at Epsom.
- Johnson keeps his world heavyweight title after a challenge by former champion Jim Jeffries. Race riots ensue.

The Arts

- The first movie made in Hollywood, "In Old California" goes on general release.
- A major breakthrough is made in talking pictures.
- Sarah Bernhardt makes her debut in music hall.
- Pre-Raphaelite painter William Holman Hunt dies.
- Stravinsky's score for the Diaghilev's ballet "The Firebird" causes a sensation.

Below:
Edward VII was almost 60 when he became the British monarch in 1901. Although, as Prince of Wales he had a reputation for being a playboy, he was very popular during his short reign. His funeral was attended by monarchs from all over Europe.

1911

World Events for 1911

- Over 1,000 troops and policemen engage 3 anarchists in a gun battle at 100 Sidney Street in London's East End.
- King George V opens his first parliament.
- Rioting erupts among strikers in British towns.
- The House of Lords gives up its struggle for supremacy over the House of Commons.
- Many die in heat waves in the USA and Britain.
- Norwegian explorer Roald Amundsen beats Scott to the South Pole.
- Employers close cotton mills leaving 300,000 workers idle.
- Russian Premier Peter Stolypin is shot dead in front of the Czar at the Kiev opera.
- Dr Sun Yat-sen leads a revolution in China to become the first President of the Chinese Republic.
- Joseph Pulitzer's will leaves an endowment for prizes for journalism.
- Corporal punishment is abolished in Denmark.

Sporting Life

- Harry Vardon wins the English Open Golf Championship.
- A record number of more than 100 male players enter the Wimbledon tennis tournament.
- Frenchman Garrigou wins the Tour de France.

The Arts

- The Irving Berlin song "Everybody's doing it" features in the Ziegfeld Follies in New York.
- The work of Van Gogh, Cezanne and Gauguin is seen in London for the first time.
- Richard Strauss's opera "Das Rosenkavalier" receives 25 curtain calls in Dresden.
- Authors and musicians are given copyright protection.
- Gustav Mahler, composer and conductor, dies aged 50.

Left:
Winston Churchill (left in the top hat), who was Home Secretary at the time, took command of the Sidney Street Seige. Three anachists resisted arrest for the murder of three policemen. Over 1,000 armed police and troops were deployed. Number 100 burned to the ground. The anachists did not surrender.

1912

World Events for 1912

- In Ulster, feelings are running high against proposals for Home Rule for Ireland.
- New Mexico becomes the 47th state of the USA.
- Dr Magitot restores a blind man's sight in a cornea graft operation.
- Captain Scott reaches the South Pole in January.
- Suffragettes smash windows in protest against the government.
- The Titanic sinks after hitting an iceberg with the loss of 1,595 lives.
- Doctors in New York condemn the use of cocaine, chloroform and ether as anaesthetics.
- Tension is mounting as war in the Balkans threatens to involve the rest of Europe.
- Woodrow Wilson becomes US President.

- Jung publishes "The Theory of Psychoanalysis".

Sporting Life

- Women's tennis outfits become shorter and easier to move in.
- Swimmer Fanny Durack of Australia wins the women's 100m freestyle in 1.22.2 in the Stockholm Olympics.
- Barnsley beat West Bromwich Albion 1-0 in the FA Cup Final replay.

The Arts

- Music hall artistes entertain the King and Queen at the first Royal Command Performance.
- "Ragtime" takes London by storm.
- "It's a long way to Tipperary" is a hit song.
- The first "Keystone Cops" movie is released.

Above:
Vincent van Gogh's paintings are probably better known today than the work of any other artist. His work was exhibited and celebrated more than 20 years after his tragic death. He suffered from mental illness as well as rejection of his work and shot himself on July 27 1890.

Left:
Believed to be indestructible, the Titanic, a British passenger ship on its maiden voyage, struck an iceberg and sank off Newfoundland. The huge loss of life was due mainly to there being insufficient lifeboats. Pictured are Cptn. E.T. Smith with victims I. Strauss and J.J. Astor.

Above:
Captain Robert Falcon Scott and his party reached the South Pole on January 18 1912, only to find that the Norwegian, Amundsen, had reached it a month earlier. On their return to base two of the party were lost, and Scott and the remaining two died in the blizzards.

1913

Right:

King George V with his nephew the German Kaiser Wilhelm. Most of the royal families of Europe are descendants of Queen Victoria. Close family ties did not prevent the Great War of 1914-1918.

World Events for 1913
- Negotiations for peace in the Balkans flounder.
- Federal income tax is introduced in the USA.
- Captain Scott and his 4 colleagues perish in the Antarctic.
- Emmeline Pankhurst is charged in connection with a bomb attack.
- Suffragette Emily Davison dies after falling under the King's horse at the Derby.
- In Germany the world's biggest airship, "Zeppelin L2" explodes killing all 28 on board.
- The Panama Canal is completed.
- Poor diet is blamed for ill health among British schoolchildren.
- Riots break out in Natal as Gandhi is jailed.
- A new 250 ft long moving assembly line for cars is unveiled at the Ford factory in Michigan.
- A couple are arrested in New York and fined for kissing in the street on Christmas Day.

Right:

Isadora Duncan had little formal training as a dancer, and devised her own free style. She toured Europe and the USA, performing in major cities. Her life was marred by tragedy.

Sporting Life
- Only 2 horses complete the Grand National at Aintree.
- Dorothea Chambers wins the Wimbledon Ladies Singles title.

The Arts
- The stolen "Mona Lisa" is recovered in Florence.
- "The Rite of Spring" by Stravinsky causes a riot at the Theatre des Champs-Elysees in Paris.
- The dancer Isadora Duncan cancels all her engagements following the death of her 2 children in a drowning accident.
- Charlie Chaplin makes his film debut in "Making a Living".

1914

World Events for 1914

- The death of the Archduke Ferdinand, shot in the Balkans, leads to war in Europe.
- Early Babylonian tablets are discovered which tell stories of Eden and a great flood.
- Doctors in London claim to have successfully treated cancer with radium.
- Civil war in Ireland over Home Rule is averted.
- Germany declares war on Russia on August 1, and on France 2 days later.
- Britain declares war on Germany on August 4.

- At Mons retreating British soldiers claim to have seen a vision of an angel.
- Turkey attacks Russian ships in the Black Sea.
- Income tax doubles in Britain to pay for the war.
- Lord Kitchener launches his recruiting campaign.
- Eastman Kodak Company announces the invention of colour photography.
- Over 100,000 British soldiers die on the battlefields of Europe.

Sporting Life

- Durbar II wins the Derby.

- Norman Brookes wins the Wimbledon Men's Singles final.
- US light heavyweight boxer Joe Jeanette beats Georges Charpentier of France to become world champion.

The Arts

- Bernard Shaw's new play "Pygmalion" is a smash hit in London.
- Wyndham Lewis, British painter and novelist, publishes the manifesto "Blast"- an attack on the smugness of English culture.
- Thomas Beecham makes his debut as a conductor.

Above:

Thousands of British men were prepared to join up and fight the war in Europe, oblivious to the reality that lay ahead of them. Over 5 million allied servicemen were killed in the conflict, and about 21 million were wounded.

World Events for 1915

- Women in Britain sign up for war work.
- The King leads a government campaign against heavy drinking.
- Stonehenge is sold at auction for £6,600.
- Albert Einstein proposes a new theory of gravity.
- Bombs are dropped on towns in eastern England from Zeppelin airships.
- The UK defends the Suez Canal against the Turks.
- German submarines attack merchant ships.
- Italy signs a secret deal to enter the war on the side of the allies. A young radical called Benito Mussolini supports the move.
- The US passenger liner the Lusitania is sunk by German submarines.
- Edith Cavell, a British nurse working in Brussels, is executed by the Germans for treason.

- In Turkey the Gallipoli offensive is called off after 8 months of disasters.
- Winston Churchill resigns from the War Cabinet and joins his regiment in France.
- The war is costing Britain £3.5m a day.

Sporting Life

- The Wimbledon Tennis Championships are suspended for the duration of the war.
- Jack Johnson's world heavyweight title is lost to Jess Willard.

- The cricketer W G Grace dies at the age of 67.

The Arts

- Charlie Chaplin stars in "The Tramp".
- The poet Rupert Brooke dies en route to the Dardanelles.
- "Pack up your troubles in your old kit bag" is a hit song.
- Richard Strauss's "Alpine Symphony" is first performed in Berlin.

Above:
Recent revelations have shown the disaters in Gallipoli were due to outdated maps and incompetent leadership.

Left:
Mata Hari, a Dutch housewife turned exotic dancer was executed for spying.

1916

World Events for 1916

- The British government votes to impose conscription.
- Wealthy people in Britain are asked to release servants to contribute to the war effort.
- Food shortages cause riots in Germany.
- Troops and a Royal Navy gunboat are sent to Dublin to quell the Easter Rising.
- US President Wilson calls for a "League of Nations" to keep world peace when the war is over.
- "Daylight saving" is introduced for the first time in the UK.
- Thousands are cut down in the first five minutes of the Battle of the Somme.
- The monk Rasputin is murdered by relatives of Czar Nicholas II.
- David Lloyd George conspires against Asquith and succeeds him as Prime Minister.
- A village policeman arrests the entire German crew of a crashed Zeppelin.
- Rising share prices in the USA make John D Rockefeller the world's first billionaire.
- 3.2 million women in Britain are employed outside the home.

Sporting Life

- The International Olympic committee meeting in Paris declares that the games will not be held until the war is over.
- The Grand National is run at Gatwick in Sussex and is won by Vermouth.

The Arts

- The Dadaist movement is born.
- Hit songs include "If you were the only girl in the world" and "Take me back to dear old Blighty".
- The American writers Jack London and Henry James die this year.
- A six week season of opera opens at Covent Garden under Sir Thomas Beecham.

Above:
At the outbreak of war in 1914 the question of home rule for Ireland had to be shelved. In 1916 there was an uprising in Dublin which resulted in the destruction of much of the city centre. A movement called Sinn Fein gathered much support.

Right:
A soldier in the trenches in the battlefield of France reads a letter from home.

1917

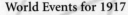

World Events for 1917

- The United States enters the war.
- The Bolsheviks seize power in Russia.
- Four men are charged with conspiracy to murder Lloyd George.
- In France restaurants can only serve 2 courses.
- British hospital ships are sunk.
- Germany helps Lenin to return to Russia to hasten the revolution and bring an end to the war.
- Countries in Central and South America declare war on Germany.
- The King orders the royal family to abandon their German names.
- Three children in Fatima, Portugal claim to have seen visions of the Virgin Mary.
- German aircraft carry out the first bombing raid on London.

- The Italian army suffers a crushing defeat at Caporetto.
- Businesses and banks call for the decimalisation of British currency.
- The Balfour Declaration promises a Jewish homeland in Palestine.

Sporting Life

- Gay Crusader wins the wartime "New Derby" at Newmarket.

The Arts

- The first jazz recording, "The Dixieland Jazz Band One-Step", is released.
- "Tom Brown's Schooldays" is the first feature film to be presented by command of the sovereign.
- "The Immigrant" starring Charlie Chaplin is released in the US.

Left:
After his victorious campaign against the Turks, General Allenby enters Jerusalem on foot.

Bottom left:
Bolshevik troops in Moscow.

Below:
A government poster urging frugality in wartime.

DON'T WASTE BREAD!

SAVE TWO SLICES EVERY DAY and Defeat the 'U' Boat

1918

World Events

- In Britain meat is rationed to 10oz per adult per week.
- In March the Bolsheviks now governing Russia sign a humiliating peace treaty with the Germans.
- The RAF is formed to consolidate revenge air attacks on Germany.
- The Czar and his family are murdered.
- More than 400 allied tanks spearhead the final thrust on German positions near Amiens. The Germans offer little resistance.
- Influenza causes millions of deaths worldwide.
- The armistice which ends the war is signed at 11 am on 11th November.
- The world grieves for "a lost generation" - over 10 million lives were lost in the war.
- The Kaiser leaves Germany in fear for his life.
- Women vote for the first time in a UK election.
- President and Mrs Wilson are entertained in London by the King and Queen.
- The Hapsburg Empire is broken up and Austria, Czechoslovakia, Hungary and an as yet unnamed Yugoslavia are born.

Sporting Life

- The grand National is won by Poethlyn.
- League football resumes in November.

The Arts

- 19 year old George Gershwin records "Swanee".
- The French composer Claude Debussy dies of cancer.
- "Till we meet again" is a hit song.

Below:
King George V with President Woodrow Wilson. This was the first time a British sovereign had welcomed a President of the United States.

Left:
German prisoners of war on the Western Front are visibly relieved at the end of hostilities.

1919

World Events
- Professor Ernest Rutherford splits the atom.
- A communist uprising in Berlin is crushed.
- The first air service links London and Paris.
- Troops under Brigadier-General Dyer open fire on demonstrators in Amritsar.
- Civil war grips Russia.
- The allies send food relief to Germany.
- President Wilson's proposals for a League of Nations is accepted.
- Alcock and Brown complete the first nonstop flight across the Atlantic.
- Lloyd George announces plans to partition Ireland.
- Nancy Astor is Britain's first woman MP.
- In Italy Mussolini forms his own fascist party.
- Eamon de Valera is elected President of Sinn Fein.
- Welsh nationalists call for a regional parliament.

Sporting Life
- Jack Dempsey wins the world heavyweight boxing championship, beating Jess Willard.

Left:
David Lloyd George became Prime Minister in Britain in 1916. He had severely criticised Prime Minister Asquith's handling of the war, and it was largely due to his leadership that the war was brought to an end in 1918. Lloyd George represented Great Britain at the Peace Conference held in Versailles.

Bottom left:
A wireless telephone transmitter and receiver developed by Marconi enabling verbal transatlantic communication.

- 20 year old Suzanne Lenglen beat the 40 year old 1914 champion Dorothea Chambers to win the Wimbledon title.
- Chelsea beats Fulham 3-1 to win the "Victory Cup".

The Arts
- Mary Pickford, Charlie Chaplin, Douglas Fairbanks and D W Griffith form the company United Artists.

- The Original Dixieland Jazz Band takes London by storm.
- The impressionist Renoir dies.
- Elgar's Cello Concerto and Holst's "The Planets" are premiered.
- The Ballets Russes visit London.

1920

Right

King George V at the funeral of the Unknown Warrior, whose tomb, at the entrance to Westmister Abbey, remains a national memorial to the millions who died in the conflict.

World Events of 1920

- War is declared between Poland and Russia.
- Women in the US win the right to vote.
- The US ban the making and selling of alcohol.
- Women are admitted to study for full degrees at Oxford University for the first time.
- Miners strike in the UK.
- Woodrow Wilson wins the Nobel Peace Prize.
- In the US, 3,000 suspected Communists are arrested.
- Martial Law is declared in Ireland as violence escalates.
- In Paris, Lloyd George receives the Grand Cross of the Legion of Honour, France's highest award.
- In London, the Communist Party of Great Britain is founded.
- In the Middle East, the state of Lebanon is created with the government at Beirut.
- The Soviet government recognises the independence of Finland.

Sporting Life

- The Olympic Games are held in Antwerp.
- Suzanne Lenglen wins the ladies' singles title at Wimbledon.
- In Britain, A. Moorhouse sets a new motor cycling record of 100 mph.
- William T. "Big Bill" Tilden II is the first American man to win the Wimbledon tennis championship.
- In football, Aston Villa beat Huddersfield in the first FA Cup Final since 1915.

The Arts

- Jazz music becomes popular.
- Douglas Fairbanks stars in "The Mark of Zorro" and sets attendance records.
- The first US commercial radio station, KDKA Pittsburg, starts broadcasting.

1921

Below:

Queen Mary was a great supporter of the interests of women. She was the first Queen of England to receive a university degree and to don the cap and gown of Oxford.

World Events of 1921

- The Communist Party is formed in China.
- In Chicago, women are fined for wearing short skirts and revealing bare arms.
- Coal rationing starts in the UK.
- Britain's first birth control clinic opens in London.
- A French engineer makes the first flight in a helicopter.
- In the US a record parachute jump from 24,400 ft is successfully made.
- Capital punishment is abolished in Sweden.
- The bubonic plague breaks out in Sydney, Australia.
- The Irish Free State is formed.
- Lenin announces New Economic Policy.
- Russia is hit by famine caused by drought and the effects of the revolution and civil war.
- Unemployment in Britain reaches 2.2 million.
- Crown Prince Hirohito becomes the Regent of Japan.
- Queen Mary is the first woman to be awarded a degree from Oxford University when she receives an honorary degree.

Sporting Life

- US athlete Charles Paddock runs the 100 metres in a world record time of 10.4 seconds.
- In cricket, Australia wins every test match in the series against England, a record.
- Baseball's World Series is won by the New York Giants, defeating rivals, the Yankees.
- In the FA Cup Final, Tottenham Hotspur beat Wolverhampton Wanderers.

The Arts

- Agatha Christie wrote her first book with the character Hercule Poirot.
- Charlie Chaplin's first full-length film, "The Kid", premieres in the US.
- Rudolph Valentino is cinema's new sensation.
- At New York's Metropolitan Museum of Art, crowds flock to see Picasso, Matisse, Manet and others.
- D.H. Lawrence publishes his novel "Women in Love".

1922

World Events of 1922

- The BBC starts broadcasting.
- The self-winding watch is invented by John Harwood.
- The Reader's Digest publishes its first edition.
- Mussolini marches on Rome and takes power.
- In Egypt, Howard Carter and Lord Carnarvon discover the tomb of the boy pharaoh Tutankhamun.
- Mahatma Gandhi is sent to jail for civil disobedience.
- In the US, the stock market boom begins.
- The Soviet states form into the USSR.
- The US signs a naval agreement with Japan.
- Tractors begin to take over from horses on farms.
- The World Court is founded at the Hague.
- Andrew Bonar Law becomes Prime Minister of Britain.
- In Russia, an estimated 33 million people are in danger of starvation.
- "Oxford Bags" are the latest fashion in trousers for British men.
- Austria declares itself bankrupt.
- The first woman US senator, Mrs W.H. Felton of Georgia is sworn in.

Sporting Life

- In golf, George Duncan scores a record round of 68 at St. Andrew's.
- Australian cricketer Jim Gregory scores the fastest test century ever against South Africa in 70 minutes.
- The Grand National is won by Music Hall, one of only three horses to complete the course.
- Suzanne Lenglen wins the Ladies' Singles title at Wimbledon.

The Arts

- Hit songs are "Limehouse Blues" and "Chicago".
- The novel "Ulysses" by James Joyce is published.
- Sound film is developed.
- The first Dracula film is released.

1922

Above:
A orchestra assembles in
a BBC studio for a live
concert radio broadcast.

Right:
The magnificent
treasures of the tomb of
Tutankhamun were
unearthed by Howard
Carter and the Earl of
Carnarvon in 1922.
Most of the tombs of
the pharoahs were
discovered and
plundered by ancient
egyptian robbers, but
this one had remained
undiscovered. This king
died aged 18 in the
14th century BC. Recent
scientific and historical
research suggest that he
was murdered.

1923

World Events of 1923

- Stanley Baldwin becomes Prime Minister of Britain.
- The Nazi party holds its first rally, in Munich.
- The biggest pig in the world weighing half a ton arrives in Sydney, Australia from New Zealand.
- A US navy airman sets a new air speed record of 259 mph.
- Tokyo, Japan is devastated by the biggest earthquake in the country's history.
- The first transatlantic wireless broadcast from the UK to the US is made.
- Germany suffers severe economic crisis—a loaf of bread in Berlin costs over 200 billion marks.
- In Australia, work begins on the Sydney Harbour Bridge.
- In the US, the city of Kalamazoo, Michigan, forbids dancers to stare into their partner's eyes.
- French and Belgium troops move into Germany to enforce war debt payments.
- London's new "super-cinema", the Tivoli, opens in the Strand.
- Lenin suffers from a stroke and resigns his leadership in Russia.
- In Australia, the first house is connected to a sewerage system in Brisbane.
- In Egypt, the Earl of Carnarvon dies from an insect bite.

Sporting Life

- The first 24 hour Le Mans Grand Prix is won by Frenchmen Lagache and Leonard.
- Suzanne Lenglen wins her fifth successive Wimbledon singles final.
- The English Channel is swum by Argentinian Enrique Tiriboschi in 16 hours and 33 minutes.
- In football, the first FA Cup Final held at Wembley Stadium is won by Bolton Wanderers.

The Arts

- US jazz singer Bessie Smith records her first song "Down-hearted Blues".
- Hit songs are "Who's Sorry Now" and "Farewell Blues".
- William Butler Yeats wins the Nobel Prize for Literature.
- T.S. Eliot's long poem "The Waste Land" is published.

1924

Sporting Life
- A seeding system for competitors is introduced at Wimbledon.
- The first winter Olympics are held in the French Alps at Chamonix.
- In football, the FA Cup Final is won by Newcastle United.

The Arts
- The film "The Ten Commandments" is released.
- George Bernard Shaw publishes "Saint Joan".
- George Gershwin's "Rhapsody In Blue" is a concert hit in New York.
- Hit songs are "All Alone" and "It Had to Be You".
- John D. Rockefeller Jr gives $1 million to the Metropolitan Museum of Art, New York.

World Events of 1924
- Kleenex introduces a new paper handkerchief in the US.
- Excavations in Egypt uncover the earliest surviving stone buildings in the world.
- Ramsay MacDonald becomes Britain's first Labour Prime Minister.
- Russian revolutionist, Lenin, dies.
- The film company MGM is founded.
- In London, Mrs Helena Normanton is the first woman barrister to practice at the Old Bailey.
- St Petersburg is renamed Leningrad after the death of Lenin.
- Ford produces its ten-millionth car.
- In Egypt, King Tutankhamun's sarcophagus is opened after more than 3,000 years.
- The first oil is discovered in Australia at Lake Bunga, Victoria.
- Albania is declared a republic.
- A broadcast from Newark, New Jersey is heard a record 9,000 miles away in Tokyo, Japan.

Far left:
Vladimir Ilyich Lenin led the Russian Revolution in 1917 and became head of the world's first communist government. His body was preserved and displayed in a tomb in Moscow.

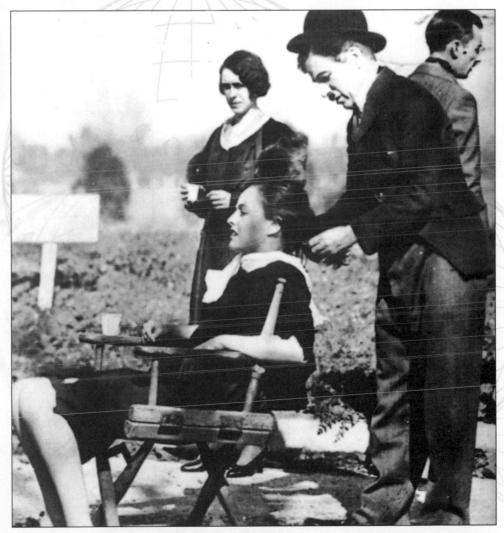

Left:
Charlie Chaplin was an outstanding film-maker and a great comic actor. He portrayed an endearing quality of sadness in his characters, paticulary 'The little tramp' which became his trademark.

1925

World Events of 1925

- Civil war rages in China.
- In South Africa blacks are banned from taking skilled jobs.
- Christiana, the capital of Norway, is renamed Oslo.
- The US state of Tennessee bans the teaching of the theory of evolution in schools.
- A US Navy seaplane sets a new record by staying in the air for 28 and a half hours.
- A new dance "The Charleston" is all the rage.
- The fossilised skull of a prehistoric ape-man is found in South Africa.
- In Italy, the Leaning Tower of Pisa is reported to be leaning more each year and is in danger of collapse.
- In the US, the Ku Klux Klan has a membership of 5 million, and terrorises religious and racial minorities.
- Chiang Kai-Shek becomes leader of China.
- In Italy, Mussolini assumes full dictatorial powers.
- Cyprus becomes a British colony.

Sporting Life

- In tennis, the US win their sixth consecutive Davis Cup title.
- In cricket, Australia score a record 600 runs in their first innings against England.
- In horse racing, Double Chance wins the Grand National at Aintree.

The Arts

- F. Scott Fitzgerald's novel "The Great Gatsby" is published.
- "Art Deco" is the new style of architecture, fashion and interior design.
- Hit songs are "Show Me the Way to Go Home", "Always" and "Manhattan".
- The first Surrealist exhibition opens in Paris.

Below:
Kitty Godfrey, the 1926 Wimbledon Ladies Singles champion is presented to the King and Queen. Their son, the Duke of York, later King George VI, played in a doubles match on the Centre Court. He and his partner lost to former champions Gore and Barratt.

1926

World Events of 1926
- The first General Strike in British history is called.
- In Paris, the Pasteur Institute discovers an anti-tetanus serum.
- In Mexico five cities built by the ancient Maya civilisation are discovered.
- Scottish inventor John Logie Baird introduces television.
- The US population reaches 115 million.
- Harry Houdini dies of a burst appendix.
- The Lebanon becomes a republic.
- Hirohito becomes Emperor of Japan.
- The League of Nations Assembly votes to admit Germany.

- In Moscow, all students are ordered to do compulsory military training.
- In India, women are allowed to stand for election to public office.
- In Rome, Mussolini reinstates the death penalty.
- The US enjoys its highest standard of living under President Coolidge.

Sporting Life
- American Gertrude Ederle is the first woman to swim the English Channel.
- Boxer Jack Dempsey loses his world heavyweight title to Gene Tunney.
- Horse racing's Grand National is won by Jack Horner.

- A new world record for the 3,000 metres of eight minutes 25 seconds is set by Finnish athlete Paavo Nurmi.

The Arts
- A.A. Milne's book "Winnie the Pooh" is published.
- Hit songs are "Bye Bye Blackbird" and "Black Bottom".
- Greta Garbo stars in the film "The Temptress".
- Duke Ellington makes his first recording.
- "The Sun Also Rises" by Ernest Hemingway is published.

Below:
Falling living standards for mining families, coupled with widespread unemployment and social bitterness led to the worst outbreak of class conflict that Britain has ever known. When the government refused to renew a subsidy to the mining industry and would not negotiate with the Trades Union Congress, a general strike was called, bringing the country to a standstill.

1927

World Events of 1927

- Greyhound racing takes Britain by storm.
- The first official Flying Doctor trip in Australia takes place.
- Pan Am launches the first international flight.
- Leon Trotsky is expelled from the Soviet Communist Party.
- A total eclipse of the sun is seen in Britain for the first time in 200 years.
- American Charles Lindbergh completes the first solo Atlantic flight, between New York and Paris.
- 52 nations meet at the Geneva economic conference.
- In Australia, the new Parliament House opens in Canberra.
- The number of telephones estimated to be in use in the UK is now 500,000.
- In the US, floods in Mississippi cover 23 square miles.
- Five year old Prince Mihai succeeds to the throne of Bucharest after the death of King Ferdinand.

Sporting Life

- In football, the FA Cup Final is won by Cardiff City after Arsenal's goalkeeper scores an own goal.
- The Harlem Globetrotters, an American basketball team, are established.
- A new world land speed record of 203.841 mph is set by Major Henry Segrave.
- In rugby, England is beaten for the first time by France, by three points to nil.
- US amateur golfer Bobby Jones wins the British Open.

The Arts

- Hit songs are "Ain't She Sweet" and "Sometimes I'm Happy".
- "The Jazz Singer", the first talking film, is released.
- 10 year old violinist, Yehudi Menuhin, amazes Parisian audiences.
- "The Bridge of San Luis Rey" by Thornton Wilder is published.
- Florenz Ziegfeld's musical "Showboat" is released.
- The Academy of Motion Picture Arts and Sciences is established.

Below left:
Charles Linbergh with his aircraft, the Spirit of St Louis.

Below:
Regent Street in London as it was in 1927.

1928

World Events of 1928

- Herbert Hoover is elected President of the United States.
- Professor Alexander Fleming discovers penicillin.
- Handshaking is banned in Rome as unhygienic.
- In Britain, women over 21 get the vote.
- The first commercial television sets go on sale in the US.
- Over 400 die as a Los Angeles dam bursts.
- 1,000 American marines are sent into Nicaragua.
- "The Flying Scotsman" train, capable of speeds over 70 mph, starts running between Edinburgh and London.
- Morris Motors launch the Morris Minor.
- In the UK, people over 65 receive their first state pensions of ten shillings a week.
- The River Thames bursts its banks, leaving hundreds homeless and causing damage to paintings at the Tate Gallery.
- In New York, nearly five million shares are sold in record trading on Wall Street.
- London Zoo acquires a 100-year-old tortoise.

Sporting Life

- The Olympic Games open in Amsterdam.
- In tennis, René Lacoste wins the men's singles final at Wimbledon.
- In football, Blackburn Rovers defeat Huddersfield Town to win the FA Cup Final.
- The Grand National at Aintree is won by Tipperary Tim.

The Arts

- Hit songs are "A Room with a View" and "Ol' Man River".
- Gershwin composes "An American in Paris".
- Charlie Chaplin stars in "The Circus".
- Laurel and Hardy appear in four films.
- Ravel composes "Bolero".
- D.H. Lawrence's novel "Lady Chatterley's Lover" is published.
- Thomas Hardy, the British author, dies.

Left:
Comedians Stan Laurel and Oliver Hardy were the screen's most popular comedy duo.

1929

World Events of 1929
- The American gangster Al Capone is jailed.
- A US army plane flies for a record 150 hours non-stop.
- Ramsay MacDonald is Britain's Prime Minister.
- The Wall Street Stock Market, New York, crashes.
- The St Valentine Day's massacre takes place in Chicago.
- Herbert Hoover is sworn in as the President of the United States.
- Border fighting breaks out between Chinese and Soviet troops in the Manchurian crisis.
- In London, Scotland Yard detectives are given radio cars for the first time.
- King Amanullah of Afghanistan restores the veil for women and abandons western dress.
- In the USSR, the working day is reduced to seven hours.
- Sir John Barrie donates his copyright fee of the story Peter Pan to the Great Ormond Street Hospital for Sick Children.
- In Rome, Mussolini bans beauty shows and contests, calling them immoral.

Sporting Life
- In football, Bolton Wanderers beat Portsmouth to win the FA Cup Final.
- Cambridge beat Oxford to win the University Boat Race.
- The Grand National at Aintree is won by a 100-1 outsider, Gregalach.
- The first Monaco Grand Prix is won by Williams of Great Britain.
- Helen Wills beats Helen Jacobs to win Wimbledon's Ladies' singles final.

The Arts
- Joan Crawford marries Douglas Fairbank Jr.
- The first exhibition of paintings by Salvador Dali opens in Paris.

- The first Academy Awards are presented in Hollywood.
- Hit songs are "Tiptoe Through the Tulips" and "Stardust".
- "A Farewell to Arms" by Ernest Hemingway is published.

Left:
The stock market in the United States, located in Wall Street New York, collapsed when the price of shares fell 40% in just a few weeks in 1929.

Above:
Salvador Dali described his work as 'hand-painted dream photographs'. He is the best known surreal artist.

1930

World Events of 1930
- The Spanish Revolution begins.
- In South Africa, white women are given the vote for the first time.
- Mahatma Gandhi is arrested by British authorities.
- In New York, scientists predict that man will land on the moon by the year 2050.
- Amy Johnson is the first woman to fly solo from Britain to Australia.
- A new planet is discovered and given the name "Pluto".
- France builds the Maginot Line.
- American Charles Lindbergh flies coast-to-coast in a record 14 hours and 45 minutes.
- Unemployment in the UK reaches 2 million.
- In Germany, Hitler's National Socialists become the country's second biggest political party.
- Britain recognises Iraqi independence.
- In Chicago, 72 people die in a heatwave.

Sporting Life
- Bobby Jones wins his third British Open Golf Championship.
- Australian cricketer Don Bradman scores a record 452 not out in a single innings.
- German boxer Max Schmeling wins the world heavyweight belt.
- In tennis, Helen Moody beats Elizabeth Ryan to win Wimbledon's Ladies' Singles Final.

The Arts
- Alfred Hitchcock's first sound film "Blackmail" is released.
- 13 year old violinist Yeheudi Menuhin plays to over 5,000 at the Albert Hall, London.
- John Gielgud plays Hamlet at the Old Vic, London.
- Noel Coward's play "Private Lives" is premiered in London.
- Greta Garbo stars in her first speaking film role in "Anna Christie".

Left:
The first soccer World Cup was won by Uruguay on home ground. Few nations entered the contest. In the semi-final, Argentina beat the USA 6-1 to face Uruguay, who won 4-2.

Right:
The German dancer, singer and actress Marlene Dietrich was signed by Paramount pictures and left her homeland for the USA in 1930. She despised the national socialism which was gaining momentum in Germany.

1931

Right:

Mahatma Gandhi left South Africa where he had campaigned for 21 years for the rights of Indian settlers, to return to his native India. He dedicated himself to the struggle for India's independence from British rule, and in March 1931, he met the Viceroy in Delhi. Gandhi was firmly opposed to violence but his peaceful demonstrations often resulted in bloodshed. He was arrested many times.

World Events of 1931
- Al Capone is jailed for 11 years for tax evasion.
- Spain is declared a republic.
- "The Star-Spangled Banner" becomes the offical US anthem.
- Traffic lights are introduced in London.
- Malcolm Campbell sets a new land speed record of 245 mph in his specially built Bluebird car.
- Economic crisis in the UK and the US causes high unemployment.
- In Italy, Mussolini makes a pact with the Vatican in Rome.
- Japan invades and captures most of Manchuria.
- King Alfonso XIII of Spain goes into exile.
- Worldwide production of cars reaches 36 million.
- In London, Oxford Street bans horses.
- In Iraq, a royal palace dating from 550 BC is discovered.
- In the UK, 28,000 people visit Whipsnade Zoo when it opens, causing chaos.
- In France, two scientists reach a height of 52,000 feet in a hot air balloon.

Sporting Life
- A baseball match is televised for the first time, in Japan.
- A new European swimming record for the 100 metres of 1 minute 10 seconds is set by Briton Joyce Cooper.
- In football, West Bromwich Albion beat Birmingham to win the FA Cup Final.

The Arts
- In Moscow, Sergei Rachmaninov's music is banned as decadent.
- "City Lights" is Charlie Chaplin's new film.
- Robert Frost wins a Pulitzer Prize for his "Collected Poems".
- The film "The Public Enemey" starring James Cagney is released.
- Hit songs are "Goodbye" and "Just One More Chance".
- Boris Karloff stars in "Frankenstein".

1932

World Events of 1932

- The BBC broadcasts for the first time from the new Broadcasting House in London.
- Franklin D. Roosevelt is elected President of the United States.
- In Australia, Sydney Harbour Bridge opens, the world's longest single-arch span.
- Vitamin C is isolated by scientists in Pittsburg, USA.
- Eamon de Valera is elected President of Ireland.
- Mahatma Gandhi is arrested in India for anti-British activism.
- In the US, Charles Lindbergh's son is kidnapped.
- In South America, nine volcanos along 400 miles of the Andes and Patagonia begin erupting.
- Ethiopian Emperor Haile Selassie abolishes slavery.

- In the UK, the Cheltenham Flyer, the world's fastest train, reaches a record average speed of 81.6 mph over 77 miles.
- In Geneva, Turkey becomes the 56th member of the League of Nations.

Sporting Life

- In golf, Gene Sarazen wins the British Open Golf Championship, the ninth successive US victory.
- In rugby, the All Blacks defeat the Wallabies by 3 tests to 1.
- The Olympic Games are held in Los Angeles.
- India play their first-ever cricket test match against England.
- Horse racing's Grand National at Aintree is won by Forbra.
- In cricket, Australia defeats South Africa by 5 tests to nil.
- Newcastle United beat Arsenal to win football's FA Cup Final.

- In billiards, Australia's Walter Lindrum makes a world record break of 4,137 points.
- Boxer Jack Sharkey beats Max Schmeling to reclaim the world heavyweight belt.
- The biggest ever sweepstake opens on the Epsom Derby with £4 million prize money.

The Arts

- Gary Cooper stars in "A Farewell to Arms".
- "Shanghai Express" opens, starring Marlene Dietrich.
- Aldous Huxley's "Brave New World" is published.
- Greta Garbo wins an Oscar for her performance in "Grand Hotel".
- Hit songs are "Love is the Sweetest Thing" and "42nd Street".
- The new Shakespeare Memorial theatre is opened in Stratford.

Below:
The Communist-run National Unemployed Workers' Movement organised thousands of jobless men to join protest marches to London to petition the government. These 'hunger marches' as they became known, were flashpoints for violent anti-government protests around the country. Many were injured and arrested.

1933

Right:

With Germany on the brink of civil war, the Nazi leader, Adolf Hitler was appointed Chancellor. Within weeks Hitler achieved his goal of total dicta-torship and his reign of terror began. As many Jews who were able fled the country, and opponents of Nazism were arrested. The first concentration camp was opened at Dachau. By the end of the year Germany had left the League of Nations.

World Events of 1933
- Prohibition ends in the US after almost 14 years.
- Japan leaves the League of Nations.
- Adolf Hitler becomes the Chancellor of Germany.
- In Berlin, the Reichstag goes up in flames.
- F.D. Roosevelt is inaugurated as America's 32nd President.
- The United States establishes diplomatic relations with the Soviet Union.
- Mahatma Gandhi is freed from jail in India after hunger striking.
- In France, the airline Air France is created.
- A flu epidemic gets worse and spreads throughout Europe.
- In Ankara, Turkey, Mustafa Kemal bans Arabic prayers and "Allah", the Arabic word for God.
- The Nazis open the first concentration camp at Dachau, near Munich.
- The Illinois Waterway is opened, linking the Great Lakes of northern US with the Gulf of Mexico.

Sporting Life
- Tennis' Davis Cup is won by Britain, ending France's seven year supremacy.
- British golfers win the Ryder Cup.
- In cricket, England defeats Australia by 4 tests to 1 in Australia.
- In baseball, the New York Giants beat the Washington Senators to win the World Series.
- Women tennis players wear shorts at Wimbledon.
- In horse racing, the Grand National at Aintree is won in record time by Kellsboro' Jack.

The Arts
- The film "King Kong" premieres in New York.
- Charlie Chaplin marries Paulette Goddard.

- Hit songs are "Smoke Gets in Your Eyes" and "Stormy Weather".
- James Joyce's "Ulysses" is legally published in the US.

- Greta Garbo stars in "Queen Christina".
- Jewish artists, writers and musicians flee Germany as Nazi's rise to power.

1934

World Events of 1934
- The first airmail service from Australia to Britain begins.
- British author H.G. Wells predicts another major war by 1940.
- "Cat's eyes" are invented.
- Hitler is voted Fuhrer of Germany.
- King Alexander of Yugoslavia is assassinated.
- The world's third-largest diamond, weighing 726 carats, is found by a poor prospector in South Africa.
- In the US, Bonnie and Clyde are shot dead.
- Fascist unrest in England is led by Sir Oswald Moseley.
- The first launderette opens in America.
- Gangster Al Capone is taken to Alcatraz Prison in the United States.
- The Monopoly board games appears for the first time.
- A Balkan pact is signed by Rumania, Greece, Yugoslavia and Turkey.

Sporting Life
- In tennis, Fred Perry becomes the first Briton to win Wimbledon for 25 years.
- In London, Cambridge win the University Boat Race in a record time of 18 minutes, 3 seconds.
- Italy win football's World Cup.
- In London, Manchester City beat Portsmouth 2-1 in the FA Cup Final at Wembley.
- In cricket, Australia defeats England by 2 tests to 1 in Australia.

The Arts
- Clark Gable wins an Oscar for his performance in the film "It Happened One Night".
- The film "The Gay Divorcee" is released starring Ginger Rogers and Fred Astaire.
- F. Scott Fitzgerald's novel "Tender is the Night" is published.
- Composer Sir Edward Elgar dies.
- "Anything Goes" by Cole Porter opens on Broadway.
- Hit songs are "I Only Have Eyes for You" and "Isle of Capri".

Left:
The murderous partnership of Bonnie and Clyde carved a trail of menace in the south western states of America for four years, robbing banks and petrol stations. They were killed when they drove at speed into an ambush in Louisiana. Their story was romanticised, and made into a movie in the 1960s.

1936

World Events of 1936
- Crystal Palace, London is burnt down.
- In England, 200 unemployed men march from Jarrow to London.
- The latest craze in the US is the new board game, Monopoly.
- Britain's super liner, The Queen Mary, sails on her maiden voyage.
- The Spanish Civil War breaks out.
- The British King, Edward VIII abdicates with American Mrs Wallis Simpson.
- American President Franklin D. Roosevelt is re-elected in a landslide victory.
- The Volkswagen motor car is launched.
- Mussolini's forces capture most of Ethiopia.
- China declares war on Japan.
- Leon Trotsky goes into exile in Mexico.
- The BBC broacasts its first full television programme.
- The first "hit-parade" appears in the American magazine "Billboard".
- 16 year old Crown Prince Farouk becomes the new King of Egypt following the death of his father King Fuad.

Sporting Life
- In football, Arsenal beat Sheffield United to win the FA Cup Final at Wembley.
- US athlete Jesse Owens wins four gold medals at the Berlin Olympics.
- British tennis player Fred Player wins the men's singles final at Wimbledon for the third successive year.
- In Britain, horse racing's Cheltenham Gold Cup is won for the fifth year in succession by Golden Miller.

The Arts
- The film "A Night at the Opera" starring the Marx brothers opens in the US.
- Charlie Chaplin's film "Modern Times" opens.
- Hit songs are "The Way You Look Tonight" and "When I'm Cleaning Windows".
- Rudyard Kipling, the British poet and writer, dies.
- In London, artist Dame Laura Knight is the first woman to be appointed to the Royal Academy.

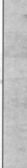

1935

World Events of 1935
- Driving tests and L-plates are introduced in the UK.
- World leaders give Hitler land in an attempt to appease him.
- Stanley Baldwin forms a National Government in Britain.
- Robert Watson Watt builds radar equipment.
- Mussolini invades Abyssinia.
- The German airforce the Luftwaffe is formed.
- A 30 mph speed limit in built-up areas comes into being in the UK.
- King George and Queen Mary celebrate their Silver Jubilee.
- US millionaire H. Hughes sets an aviation speed record of 347.5 mph.
- In Britain, Penguin Books publish their first paperbacks.
- T.E. Lawrence – Lawrence of Arabia – dies.
- An earthquake on the Chinese island of Formosa kills over 2,000.
- American scientists isolate vitamin E.

Sporting Life
- US athlete Jesse Owens breaks five world records in a day.
- In boxing, James J. Braddock wins the world heavyweight title.
- Horse racing's Grand National, held at Aintree, is won by Reynoldstown.
- In England, Sheffield Wednesday beat West Bromwich Albion to win the FA Cup Final at Wembley.

The Arts
- 19 year old Vivien Leigh signs a record £50,000 film contract.
- The film "Mutiny on the Bounty" starring Clark Gable is released.
- Gershwin's opera "Porgy and Bess" opens in New York.
- Hit songs are "Blue Moon" and "Red Sails in the Sunset".
- Greta Garbo stars in "Anna Karenina".

1937

World Events of 1937
- The former King Edward VIII marries Mrs Wallis Simpson.
- George VI is crowned.
- The world's longest suspension bridge, the Golden Gate Bridge, is opened in San Francisco.
- Chamberlain becomes Prime Minister of Britain.
- The first Butlin holiday camp opens.
- The Hindenburg, a giant airship, explodes.
- A minimum wage for women is ordered by US courts.
- Britain signs naval agreements with Germany and Russia.
- In New York, stock prices fall on Wall Street, starting a recession.
- A new rescue service is introduced in Britain—dial 999 for help.
- Malcolm Campbell sets a new water speed record of 129 mph.
- The Turkish government announces its plans to conscript women from 16 to 60 in time of war.

Sporting Life
- The first Australian women cricketers tour England.
- Horse racing's Grand National celebrates its centenary, and is won by Royal Mail.
- In boxing, Joe Louis defeats James J. Braddock to win the world heavyweight title.
- In English football, Sunderland beat Preston North End to win the FA Cup Final.

The Arts
- Karen Blixen's novel "Out of Africa" is published.
- Dancer Margot Fonteyn debuts in "Giselle".
- "Snow White", Disney's first full colour cartoon, is released.
- American composer George Gershwin dies.
- Child star Shirley Temple earns $100,000 a film.

Opposite page:
The romance between the heir to the British throne and Mrs Wallis Simpson, an American divorcee, remained a well kept secret until George V died in 1936. King Edward VIII was never crowned, choosing instead to marry Mrs Simpson. They were given the titles Duke and Duchess of Windsor and went to live in France.

Centre:
The 1936 Olympic Games held in Berlin were considered to be a propaganda coup for the Nazi regime of Adolf Hitler. However, the victories of black American athlete Jesse Owens presented the Fuhrer with an embarassing problem. Believing firmly in Aryan supremacy, Hitler refused to shake hands with Owen.

Left:
The Civil War in Spain erupted when the army, led by General Franco, rose against the Spanish Republican government.

1938

World Events of 1938
- Japan conquers much of China.
- Hitler moves into Austria and Czechoslovakia.
- Australia is 150 years old.
- A new comic strip, "Superman", starts in the US.
- Gas masks are issued in Britain.
- Eskimos in the Arctic complain of a heatwave. It is 67°F (19°C).
- US breaks diplomatic ties with Germany.
- The Spanish Civil War rages.

- In Britain, the police recommend that all bicycles should be fitted with rear lights.
- In London, Scotland Yard announces that it is to start using police dogs.
- A British locomotive, the Mallard, sets a new world record speed for steam engines of 126 miles per hour.
- In Britain, Thomas Cook offers an eight day holiday on the French Riviera for £8/17/6d.

Sporting Life
- In England, Helen Wills Moody wins her eighth Wimbledon singles title.
- In England, the FA Cup Final is covered live by television for the first time.

- In the final test, England's cricketers beat the Australians by a record innings and 579 runs.
- The Grand National at Aintree is won by Battleship.

The Arts
- A radio production of "War of the Worlds" causes widespread panic in the US.
- Gracie Fields is awarded a CBE.
- J.R.R. Tolkein's novel "The Hobbit" is published.
- Mickey Rooney stars in "Love Finds Andy Hardy".
- The film "You Can't Take it with You" starring Jimmy Stewart is released.

1939

World Events of 1939
- The Rockefeller Center in New York is completed.
- The Spanish Civil War ends.
- World War II is declared.
- Air raid shelters are distributed free to London homes.
- Nylon stockings go on sale in the US for the first time.
- Women and children are evacuated from London.
- The Royal Melbourne Hospital opens.
- President Franklin D. Roosevelt declares US neutrality as war in Europe breaks out.
- King George VI and Queen Elizabeth visit New York's World Fair.
- The King of Iraq is killed in an accident and is succeeded by four-year-old Emir Faisal.
- Germany launches its 35,000 ton battleship, the Bismarck.
- Spain leaves the League of Nations.

Sporting Life
- Baseball is televised for the first time, in the US.

- In tennis, Australia wins the Davis Cup for the first time.
- In British football, Portsmouth beat Wolverhampton Wanderers 4-1 to win the FA Cup Final.
- In England, there is no cricket due to the war.

The Arts
- The film "The Hunchback of Notre Dame" starring Charles Laughton is released.
- "The Grapes of Wrath" by John Steinbeck is published.
- John Wayne stars in the film "Stagecoach".
- Glenn Miller records the song "In the Mood".
- "The Wizard of Oz" is premieried and makes Judy Garland a star.
- "Gone With the Wind" is released and goes on to win 10 Oscars.
- Hit songs are "I'll Never Smile Again", "Over the Rainbow" and "Washing on the Siegfried Line".

1940

World Events of 1940
- World War II rages.
- Winston Churchill becomes Prime Minister of Britain.
- Winston Churchill renames the Local Defence Volunteers the Home Guard.
- In Tibet, the 5-year-old Dalai Lama is enthroned.
- In London, Buckingham Palace is bombed but the King and Queen are unhurt.
- A 12,000-year-old Aboriginal skull is found at Keilor in Victoria, Australia.
- In England the fascist leader Oswald Moseley is put into prison.
- In Italy, Mussolini orders the mobilisation of all Italians over the age of 14.
- In the Dunkirk evacuation 338,000 allied troops are rescued from the beaches of France.
- German troops invade much of Europe.
- Italy declares war on the UK and France.
- Penicillin is developed as an antibiotic.
- Prehistoric cave paintings are discovered at Lascaux in France.
- The Battle of Britain rages in the skies above southern England.

Sporting Life
- In Britain, there is no test cricket due to the war.
- In Britain, the Jockey Club cancels this year's Derby.
- The World Snooker Championship is won by Horace Lindrum.
- In baseball, the Cincinnati Reds defeat the Detroit Tigers 4-3 in the World Series.

The Arts
- Charlie Chaplin's new film "The Great Dictator" arrives in Britain.
- Hit songs are "When You Wish Upon a Star", "You are my Sunshine" and "A Nightingale Sang in Berkeley Square".
- Ernest Hemingway's novel of the Spanish Civil War, "For Whom the Bell Tolls", is published.
- Walt Disney's "Fantasia" and "Pinocchio" open.

"LET US GO FORWARD TOGETHER"

Above:
Winston Churchill's leadership during the war, depicted in this recruitment poster, inspired and encouraged the nation.

1941

Right:

With London under the threat of German air strikes, mothers were urged to send their children out of the city to be billetted in homes in the country. Few such children have fond memories of their war years.

World Events of 1941

- On July 6th London has its sunniest day of the century with 15 hours 48 minutes of sunshine.

- The Japanese attack the American naval base Pearl Harbour.
- Germans order Jews to wear the Star of David.

- The German battleship Bismarck, claimed to be unsinkable, is sunk by the Royal Navy.
- Britain and Australia declare war on Japan.
- Australia's largest ship, the QE2, takes troops overseas.
- In London, publication of the Communist paper Daily Worker is banned by the government.
- The war costs Britain £11 million a day.
- In the UK, all single women between 20 and 30 are called up to help the war effort.
- Rudolf Hess, Hitler's deputy, parachutes into Scotland.
- Germany invades Russia.
- In England, the goverment's proposal that theatres are opened on Sunday is rejected by MPs.

Sporting Life

- Skipton wins the Melbourne Cup.
- US baseball legend Lou Gehrig dies.
- Baseball star Joe DiMaggio hits safely in a record 56 games in a row.

The Arts

- In Britain, the radio becomes the main source of entertainment.
- German actress Marlene Dietrich becomes a US citizen.
- Noel Coward's play "Blithe Spirit" opens.
- Hit songs are " White Cliffs of Dover", "Blues in the Night", "I Don't Want to Set the World on Fire" and "Chattanooga Choo-Choo".
- The film "The Road to Zanzibar" starring Bob Hope, Bing Crosby and Dorothy Lamour opens in New York.
- Bertolt Brecht's play "Mother Courage" is premiered in Zurich.

1942

World Events of 1942
- The first US troops arrive in Europe.
- In Britain, women are encouraged to use soot for eye makeup, beetroot juice for lipstick and to pencil-in stocking seams with gravy browning.
- In one raid, more than a thousand RAF planes attack Cologne, Germany.
- In Britain, ration coupons are introduced for clothes.
- In America, the goverment puts 100,000 Japanese-Americans into detention.
- The Battle of the Coral Sea begins and is won by US forces.
- The Commonwealth government introduces pensions for widows.
- Singapore falls to the Japanese.
- In Australia, Darwin is attacked by Japanese aircraft and 11 ships are sunk.
- Mahatma Gandhi is arrested in India.
- The US Navy signs up its first ever black recruits.
- The Battle of El Alamein takes place in North Africa between Germany and the Allies.
- The BBC starts broadcasting a daily news bulletin to the French Resistance in morse code.

Sporting Life
- Softball is introduced to Australia.
- Boxer Joe Louis knocks out Max "Buddy" Baer to retain the world heavy weight crown.
- There is no test cricket due to the war.
- In Australia, Cambridge are the Rugby League Premiers.

The Arts
- Bing Crosby records "White Christmas".
- In London, Epstein's new sculpture "Jacob and the Angel" goes on show.
- Walt Disney's "Bambi" is released.
- Humphrey Bogart and Ingrid Bergman star in "Casablanca".
- Hit songs are "We'll Meet Again" and "White Christmas".
- Ronald Reagan stars in the film "King's Row".

1943

World Events of 1943

- Howard Florey discovers how to extract penicillin from mould.
- Mussolini, the Italian Fascist dictator, falls from power.
- The King of England is reported to have a part-time job in a munitions factory.
- President Roosevelt appoints General Dwight D. Eisenhower supreme commander of the Allied invasion of Western Europe.
- In Britain, the price of drinks goes up and a 100% tax on luxuries is introduced in the budget.
- In Rome, the Fascist party is abolished.
- The Allies hold a conference in Casablanca.
- Britain's largest charitable trust, the Nuffield Foundation, is created by Lord Nuffield, with a gift of £10 million.
- At Christmas, the British government says there are only enough turkeys for one family in ten.
- The Ruhr Dam in Germany is destroyed by the RAF.
- In London, the Court of Appeal rules that savings from housekeeping money belong to the husband.
- Italy surrenders to the Allies.
- Part-time work for women aged 18-45 becomes compulsory in the UK.

Sporting Life

- In Britain, Ascot holds its first wartime race meeting.
- There is no cricket in Australia due to the war.
- The New York Yankees win baseball's World Series.
- The Melbourne Cup winner is Dark Felt.

The Arts

- British author and illustrator Beatrix Potter dies.
- The film "Casablanca" wins an Oscar.
- "Being and Nothingness" by Jean-Paul Sartre is published.
- British actors vote in favour of opening theatres on Sundays.
- The musical "Oklahoma!" sets records in Broadway.
- Hit songs are "You'll Never Know", "Oh, What a Beautiful Morning" and "My Heart and I".

1944

World Events of 1944

- D-Day, 8th May: Allied troops land in Normandy in the world's biggest invasion in military history.
- Hitler survives an assassination attempt.
- Fossils and tools used in the Old Stone Age, 250,000 years ago, are discovered in the Great Rift Valley, Kenya.
- In America, the cost of living increases by nearly one-third.
- Decca issue the first hi-fi records.
- Vietnam declares independence.
- Japanese prisoners of war attempt a mass breakout at Cowra, Australia.
- DNA is discovered by scientists at the Rockefeller Institute in New York.
- Clothing restrictions are lifted in Britain.
- In Britain the ban on women teachers marrying is lifted.
- The RAF drop a record 4,500 tons of bombs in a single raid on Germany, France and Belgium.
- Flying bombs known as doodlebugs, Hitler's secret weapon, attack south-east Britain and the second mass wartime evacuation of children from London begins.

Sporting Life

- In Britain, Oxford wins the Boat Race.
- In Australia, Sirius wins the Melbourne Cup.
- Sport worldwide is affected by the war.
- The baseball World Series is won by St. Louis Cardinals.

The Arts

- "Going My Way" with Bing Crosby wins four Oscars.
- Laurence Olivier stars in "Henry V".
- Hit songs are "Mairzy Doats" and "There Goes that Song Again".
- Tennessee Williams' play "The Glass Menagerie" opens.
- Glenn Miller, American band leader, dies in a plane crash.

Left:
As the allied troops swept through France, the occupying Germans were forced to lsurrender. The war in Europe was brought to an end 12 months after the Normandy landings.

1945

World Events of 1945

- World War II ends.
- The World Bank is established.
- In Britain over 43,000 dockers unofficially strike over pay.
- The United Nations Educational, Scientific and Cultural Organisation (UNESCO) is founded.
- American President Roosevelt dies at the age of 63, on the eve of victory.
- Child benefit is introduced in Britain.
- Germany is divided into four parts and the Allies occupy Berlin.
- Hitler commits suicide.
- The United Nations is founded.
- Home Rule is proposed for India.
- A B-52 US bomber hits the Empire State Building.
- The city of Hiroshima in Japan is destroyed by an atomic bomb.
- The Nuremberg trials for German war criminals begin.
- In Britain, Labour has a landslide victory in the general election.

Sporting Life

- Throughout the world, sport is affected by the war.
- American army sergeant Frank A. Parker wins the US Lawn Tennis singles.
- The baseball World Series is won by the Detroit Tigers.
- Jackie Robinson is the first African-American signed to major-league baseball.

The Arts

- Frank Lloyd Wright designs the Guggenheim Museum in New York.
- The Louvre art gallery reopens in Paris.
- George Orwell's "Animal Farm" is published.
- "Brideshead Revisited" by Evelyn Waugh is published.
- Hit songs are "My Guy's Come Back", "Cruising Down the River" and "We'll Gather Lilacs in the Spring".

Right:
There was celebration and dancing in the streets of London on VE Day (Victory in Europe Day), 8 May 1945.

1946

World Events of 1946
- Civil war breaks out in China.
- 50,000 British GI brides rejoin their soldier husbands in America.
- Bananas are back in Britain for the first time since 1939.
- There is a world food shortage.
- In Italy, women are given the right to vote.
- In America, President Harry Truman sets up the Central Intelligence Group.
- The jitterbug, the new dance craze from America, hits Britain.
- The monarchy ends in Italy.
- IBM produce an advanced calculator.
- The first sub-surface atomic explosion is detonated at Bikini Atoll, in the Pacific.
- In London, the Food Ministry issues a recipe for squirrel pie.
- Hindu-Moslem riots break out in India, and thousands die.
- British European Airways is created.

Sporting Life
- League football returns to England for the first time since 1939.
- Australia, with Donald Bradman as captain, retains the Ashes in the MCC tour.
- In the shortest recorded boxing fight in history, Couture beats Walton with one punch in 10.5 seconds.
- The US team win the Davis Cup tennis trophy against Australia.
- In Britain, the first Grand National since 1940 is won by Lovely Cottage.

The Arts
- Jimmy Stewart stars in "It's a Wonderful Life".
- The British Arts Council is instituted.
- The first Cannes Film Festival opens in France.
- Hit songs are "A Gal in Calico" and "It's a Pity to Say Goodnight".
- "The Best Years of our Lives" wins seven Oscars for its portrayal of post-war life.
- "Annie Get Your Gun" is premiered on Broadway.

1947

Right:
On November 20 1947 Princess Elizabeth, the heir to the throne, was married to her distant cousin Prince Philip, Duke of Edinburgh, formerly Lieutenant Philip Mountbatten.
She wore a gown embroidered with pearl and beaded flowers designed by Norman Hartnell.

World Events of 1947
- Chuck Yeager, an American test pilot, became the first man to travel faster than sound, at over 600 mph.
- Over 8,500,000 Hindu and Moslem refugees leave India and cross the Indo-Pakistan border in four months – the largest migration in history
- Princess Elizabeth marries Prince Philip.
- British rule in India ends.
- Australia's immigration boom begins.
- A record 50,000 divorces a year are taking place in Britain.
- 28 inches of snow falls in New York on one day as a blizzard sweeps through the city.
- Radiocarbon dating is introduced.

- In Britain, pleasure motoring and foreign holidays are banned.
- Russia explodes her first atomic bomb.
- Sightings of "flying saucers" are reported in the US.
- The first transistor is produced.
- British women are asked to save cloth by wearing shorter skirts.

Sporting Life
- In football, Charlton Athletic beat Burnley 1-0 to win the FA Cup.
- In cricket, Australia defeats England by 3 tests to nil.
- Denis Compton ends the cricket season by scoring a record 3,816 runs and 18 centuries.

- A 100-1 outsider, Caughoo, wins the Grand National.
- Jack Kramer wins the men's singles final at Wimbledon.

The Arts
- The Edinburgh Festival is launched.
- Tennesse Williams' play "A Streetcar Named Desire" is premiered.
- Hit songs are "Maybe it's Because I'm a Londoner" and "They Say it's Wonderful".
- The musical "Annie Get Your Gun" opens in London.
- French novelist André Gide wins the Nobel Prize for Literature

1948

World Events of 1948
- Mahatma Gandhi is assassinated in New Delhi, India.
- United States' scientists warn that the world is outgrowing its food supply.
- The National Health Service is launched in Britain.
- Commonwealth citizens are offered British passports.
- The State of Israel is created.
- Floods in Oregon, America leave 60,000 people homeless.
- The Vickers Viscount, the world's first turbine-propellor aircraft, makes its maiden flight.
- The foundation stone of the Aswan Dam in Egypt is laid by King Farouk.
- The World Health Organisation is established.
- Long playing records are made.
- Russians blockade Berlin so the Allies organise the airlift.
- An American survey published finds that 56% of American men have been unfaithful to their wives.

Sporting Life
- The Olympic Games are held in London.
- Henry Cotton wins the British Open Golf Championship for the third time.
- A 12 year old jockey, Lester Piggott, is Britain's youngest race winner.
- Americans win 38 medals at the Olympics.
- Manchester United beat Blackpool 4-2 in the FA Cup Final.
- In Britain, the Aga Khan's horse My Love wins the Derby.

The Arts
- T.S. Eliot is awarded both the Nobel Prize and the Order of Merit.
- Laurence Olivier stars in the film "Hamlet".
- Hit songs are "It's Magic" and "On a Slow Boat to China".
- American artist Jackson Pollock causes a sensation in New York with his new technique called Action Painting.

Below:
Before the Berlin Wall separated east from west all citizens were able to move freely in and out of all zones. Those living in the Soviet sector did not embrace communism overnight, and huge demonstrations were held against the Russian blockade. Even though goods could not be brought in to the western zones across East Germany the allied air lift of food and essential supplies successfully thwarted Russian attempts to force the allies to accept their plans for the future of Germany.

1949

World Events of 1949
- The Berlin blockade is lifted.
- The North Atlantic Treaty is signed.
- Eire is proclaimed the Republic of Ireland.
- Mao Tse-tung proclaims the People's Republic of China.
- Clothes rationing ends in Britain.
- In London, starlings sitting on the minute hand of Big Ben, make the clock lose four and a half minutes, the slowest it has gone for 90 years.
- Nehru becomes the Prime Minister of India.
- 100,000 migrants from Britain arrive in Australia.
- The State of Vietnam is established.
- The USSR tests its first nuclear bomb.
- The world's first jet airliner makes its maiden flight.
- Anti-communist hysteria sweeps through the US.
- NATO is formed by 12 nations.
- South Africa establishes the apartheid regime.
- East Germany becomes the German Democratic Republic, the West is the German Federal Republic.

Sporting Life
- In Britain, the Grand National at Aintree is won by Russian Hero.
- Italy's national football team are killed in an air crash.
- Louise Brough beats Mrs Du Pont in the Wimbledon women's singles final.
- American boxer Joe Louis retires with a near-perfect record.
- In Britain, Wolverhampton Wanderers beat Leicester City to win the FA Cup final.

The Arts
- Dramatisation of H.G. Wells' "War of the Worlds" causes panic in Ecuador.
- The entire Tate Gallery in London is reopened for the first time since 1939.
- "Hamlet" is released on film and wins 5 Oscars.
- Arthur Miller wins a Pulitzer Prize for his play "Death of a Salesman".
- Hit songs are "Rudolph The Red Nosed Reindeer" and "Riders in the Sky".
- The musical "South Pacific" opens in America.

Left:
With the help of Soviet Communists, Mao Tse Tung's army won a victory over the Nationalists in 1949 and he became the Chairman of the People's Republic of China.

1950

World Events of 1950

- The population of the US is over 150 million.
- The Korean War breaks out.
- The first kidney transplant is carried out in the US.
- This year is the centenary of the bowler hat.
- The "Eagle" comic is launched in Britain.
- Customs officers in Liverpool seize smuggled nylon stockings with a black market value of £80,000, after raiding a transatlantic liner.
- A new law in China bans polygamy, infanticide and the marriage of children.
- A survey claims that only 46% of British households have a bathroom.
- The United Nations building opens in New York.
- In Paris, a bill is passed curbing the sale of Coca-Cola.
- Petrol and soap rationing in the UK ends.
- America is in the grips of "McCarthysim".

Sporting Life

- Britain wins eight gold medals in the European Games held in Belgium.
- England footballers lose 1-0 to the United States in the first round of the World Cup.
- In tennis, Australia beats the United States to win the Davis Cup.
- British athlete Roger Bannister runs the mile in a record 4 minutes 1.48 seconds.

The Arts

- The film "All About Eve", starring Bette Davis and Marilyn Monroe, is nominated for a record 14 Oscars.
- Hit songs are "I've Got a Lovely Bunch of Coconuts" and "Mona Lisa".
- Drive-in movies increase in popularity in the US.
- "Guys and Dolls" opens on Broadway.
- Frank Sinatra makes his London debut at the London Palladium.

Left:
The film actor and popular singer Frank Sinatra meeting the secretary of his fan club in Britain during one of his London visits.

1951

World Events of 1951

- Winston Churchill becomes Prime Minister again at the age of 77.
- The US tests the H-bomb and nuclear power.
- Footprints of the "Yeti", the "Abominable Snowman" are allegedly found.
- The Korean War rages.
- Jordan's King Abdullah is assassinated at a Jerusalem mosque.
- The first Miss World contest is held.
- In New York, Julius and Ethel Rosenberg are found guilty of wartime espionage and sentenced to death.
- British spies Burgess and Maclean defect to Russia.
- The first colour television appears in the US.
- The Waverly Council in Sydney, Australia bans the bikini on its beaches.
- Libya, backed by the United Nations, gains independence.
- Britain's first atomic bomb is tested in the Indian Ocean.

Sporting Life

- In cricket, Len Hutton scores his 100th century.
- In tennis, Frank Sedgman becomes the first Australian to win the United States Open.
- The first Asian games open, in New Delhi.
- Le Mans Grand Prix, France is won by Briton Peter Walker, in a Jaguar.
- In Britain, the University Boat Race is called off after the Oxford boat sinks.

The Arts

- Swedish actress Greta Garbo becomes a US citizen.
- Hit songs are "Shall we Dance?" and "If".
- Humphrey Bogart and Katherine Hepburn star in "The African Queen
- The Royal Festival Hall, London is opened by the King.
- Benjamin Britten's opera "Billy Budd" premieres in the UK.

Right:
Senator Joseph R McCarthy, an active anti-communist, accused US government agencies and officials of 'un-American activities'. He became Chairman of the Senate Government Operations Committee, but his actions, referred to a 'witch-hunts' have been discredited.

1952

World Events of 1952
- Eisenhower is elected President of the United States.
- 16,000 people escape from East to West Berlin in one month.
- America explodes the hydrogen bomb.
- King George VI dies.
- The diary of Anne Frank is published.
- In Cyprus, Greeks attack British forces and Turkish minority.
- Britain develops its first atomic bomb.
- Crown Prince Hussein becomes King of Jordan at the age of 17.
- The Nobel Peace Prize is awarded to Albert Schweitzer.
- President Truman officially ends the war in the Pacific.
- The world's first atomic-powered submarine is launched in the US.
- The US liner "United States" crosses the Atlantic in a record three days, ten hours and 40 minutes.
- Eva Peron, the Argentinian politician, dies.

Sporting Life
- The Olympic Games are held in Helsinki.
- 17 year old Maureen "Little Mo" Connolly wins Wimbledon.
- The Australian tennis team wins the Davis Cup.
- In cricket, Australia defeats the West Indies 4 Tests to 1.
- The United States win 43 gold medals at the Olympic Games.

The Arts
- "East of Eden" by John Steinbeck is published.
- It is the world premiere of Charlie Chaplin's film "Limelight".
- Samuel Beckett publishes "Waiting for Godot".
- Opera singer Maria Callas is "discovered" at the Royal Opera House, Covent Garden.
- Agatha Christie's latest play "The Mousetrap" opens in London.
- Hit songs are "I'm Singing in the Rain" and "It Takes Two to Tango".
- Ernest Hemingway's novel "The Old Man and the Sea" is published.

Left:
Maria Callas, pictured here with Tito Gobi and Renato Cioni, stunned the audience at Covent Garden when she made her debut singing the title role in Bellini's "Norma".

1953

World Events of 1953

- Sir Winston Churchill wins the Noble Prize for literature.
- Joseph Stalin dies.
- A vaccine against polio is successfully tested.
- Everest is conquered by Edmund Hillary and Sherpa Tensing.
- The Korean War ends.
- Britain recognises the Republic of Egypt.
- The coronation of Queen Elizabeth II is held.
- Stiletto heels are the latest fashion in footwear.
- John F. Kennedy marries Jacqueline Bouvier.
- The new Ford Popular is launched; at £390 it is the cheapest car on the British market.
- Eisenhower is inaugurated as President of the US.
- A record 30,031 new houses are built in one month in the UK.
- The US Supreme Court considers banning racial segregation in schools.

Sporting Life

- In England, football star Stanley Matthews helps Blackpool win their first ever FA Cup final.
- In tennis, 18-year-old Ken Rosewall wins the Australian Singles Title.
- Jim Peters is the first man to run a marathon in under 2 hours 20 minutes.
- English cricketers regain the Ashes from the Australians after 20 years.
- American tennis player Maureen Connolly wins the Grand Slam.
- In football, Arsenal win the League Championship for a record seventh time.

The Arts

- In Paris, Samuel Beckett's play "Waiting for Godot" is premiered.
- Ernest Hemingway wins a Pulitzer Prize for "The Old Man and the Sea" and "Picnic".

- Hit songs are "Diamond's are a Girl's Best Friend", "How Much is that Doggy in the Window?" and "I Love Paris".

1954

Left and far left:
Queen Elizabeth II was crowned in Westmister Abbey on June 2 1953. The procession and entire ceremony were broadcast live on television.

Far left, bottom:
Thousands lined the procession route and those who wanted a good place camped overnight in the rain.

Right:
Roger Bannister broke the British record for the mile in 1953, and made his attempt to run the distance in under 4 minutes at Oxford. His first record was broken by John Landy a few weeks later, but Bannister took the record again later that year at the Empire Games in Canada.

World Events of 1954
- Australia's population reaches 9 million.
- After 14 years, all rationing ends in the UK.
- Colonel Nasser takes power in Egypt and the British give up their occupation.
- In Rome, Pope Pius XII warns that television is a potential threat to family life.
- Marilyn Monroe marries ex-baseballer Joe DiMaggio.
- Britain's rabbit population is in danger of being wiped out by the virus myxomatosis.
- American evangelist Billy Graham tours Britain.
- Queen Elizabeth II is the first reigning monarch to visit Australia.
- The McCarthy "witch hunts" begin in the US.
- In America, Nautilus, the first nuclear submarine, is launched.
- Mao Tse-tung is re-elected as leader of China.
- The first pre-recorded tapes are available in Britain.
- A new board game, Scrabble, is launched.
- The Mau-Maus rebel in Kenya.

Sporting Life
- American tennis player Maureen Connolly wins her third successive Wimbledon ladies singles title.
- British student Roger Bannister is the first man to run a mile in under four minutes in 3 minutes, 59.4 seconds.
- 24 year old Australian golfer Peter Thomson becomes the youngest ever winner of the British Open Championship.
- British jockey Lester Piggott becomes the youngest Derby winner.

The Arts
- The first Newport Jazz Festival stars Ella Fitzgerald and Dizzy Gillespie.
- Bill Haley and the Comets top the charts with their latest record, "We're Gonna Rock Around the Clock".
- Elvis Presley records his first song, "That's All Right Mama".
- William Golding's novel "Lord of the Flies" is published.

1955

Right:
The screen idol James Dean made only three films before he was tragically killed in a road accident at the age of 24.

World Events of 1955
- Disneyland opens in California, America at a cost of $17m.
- Albert Einstein, the scientist dies at the age of 76.
- In the US, Donald Campbell sets a new water speed record of 216.2 mph in his speedboat Bluebird.
- Nautilus, the first atomic submarine, leaves dock.
- James Dean dies in a car accident at the age of 24.
- British MPs vote to keep the death penalty.
- Germany joins NATO.
- Winston Churchill resigns as Prime Minister of Britain and is replaced by Anthony Eden.
- In a dispute at Fleet Street, The Times stops publication for the first time in 170 years.
- The MacDonalds chain of restaurants is formed in the US.
- Civil war breaks out in Vietnam.

Sporting Life
- Newcastle United play in a record tenth FA Cup final, beating Manchester City.
- The Grand National is won by Mrs Welman's horse Quare Times.
- In tennis, Australia defeat the US to win the Davis Cup.
- Louise Brough wins her fourth women's singles championship at Wimbledon.
- The first floodlit international football match is played at Wembley, between England and Spain.
- In cricket, England defeats Australia 3 tests to 1.

The Arts
- Marion Anderson becomes the first black singer to perform at the Metropolitan Opera House, New York.
- Tennessee Williams' play "Cat on a Hot Tin Roof" is premiered in New York.
- "Rebel Without a Cause" opens, James Dean's last film.
- Hit songs are "The Yellow Rose of Texas" and "Sixteen Tons".
- Barry Humphries' character "Edna Everage" makes her stage debut.
- Marilyn Monroe stars in "The Seven Year Itch".

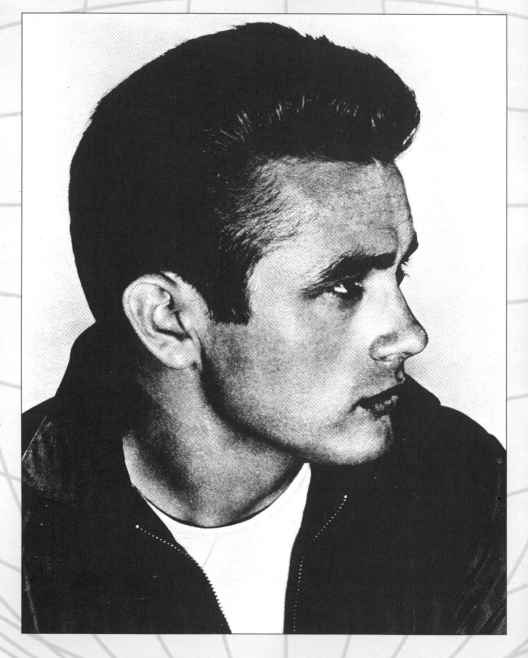

1956

World Events of 1956
- Martin Luther King campaigns for desegregation.
- Israel invades Egypt.
- Prince Rainier II weds the actress Grace Kelly.
- The Suez Crisis between England and Egypt rages.
- Soviet troops invade Hungary to quell the revolution.
- The US drops the first H-bomb from a plane over Bikini Atoll in the Pacific.
- In London, the Duke of Edinburgh announces an award scheme for young people.
- Japan joins the United Nations.
- The import and export of heroin is banned in Britain.
- An oral vaccine against polio is perfected by Dr Albert Sabin in America.
- Fidel Castro leads an uprising against the Cuban government.
- In the US the Supreme Court bans segregated bus seating.
- In Paris, French Morocco is granted its independence.

Sporting Life
- In cricket, England defeats Australia 2 tests to 1.
- The 16th Olympic games opens in Melbourne, Australia.
- Jim Laker, the English cricketer, takes 19 wickets in the test against Australia.
- British racing driver Stirling Moss wins his second Grand Prix in Monaco.
- In football, Real Madrid win the first European Cup.
- Lew Hoad beats Ken Rosewall to win the men's singles final at Wimbledon.

The Arts
- In London, the National Youth Theatre is founded.
- The musical "My Fair Lady" opens in New York.
- John Osborne's new play "Look Back in Anger" opens.
- Eurovision Song Contest is first televised.
- Rex Harrison and Julie Andrews star in "My Fair Lady".
- Hit songs are "Blue Suede Shoes" and "Que Sera, Sera".
- Elvis Presley stars in "Love Me Tender".

Below:
Hungary was occupied by Soviet troops in 1945, and became a communist country. In October 1956 the communists were overthrown in a revolution, but this was quickly thwarted when theSoviet army invaded the country again and it was restored to communist rule.

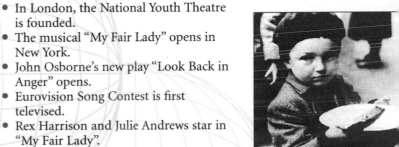

1957

World Events of 1957
- 2,000 people a week are reported to be emigrating from the UK to the Commonwealth.
- In Pretoria, South Africa drops "God Save the Queen" as its national anthem.
- The Gold Coast is granted its independence, and renamed Ghana.
- In America, San Francisco is hit by the worst tremors since the great earthquake of 1906.
- A tidal wave and hurricane kills over 500 people in Louisana and Texas.
- Britain conducts its first nuclear weapon tests in Western Australia.
- Harold McMillan becomes the new Prime Minister of Britain.
- The European Common Market, to become the European Economic Community (EEC) is created.
- Russia launches Sputnik-I, the first space satellite, the second launch includes a dog, Laika.
- Elvis Presley is called up to join the army.
- The world's longest suspension bridge, the Mackinac Straits Bridge, Michigan is constructed.
- The Asian Flu epidemic breaks out in Australia.
- Olaf V becomes the King of Norway.

Sporting Life
- In football, Real Madrid win the European Cup Final.
- American Althea Gibson becomes the first black Wimbledon champion.
- The Australian Soccer Federation is founded.
- In tennis, Australia beats the US to win the Davis Cup .
- In Britain, the Grand National is won by Sundew.

The Arts
- "The Bridge on the River Kwai" wins Oscars
- Mariln Monroe stars in "The Prince and the Showgirl".
- French novelist Albert Camus wins the Nobel Prize for Literature.
- The Royal Ballet is founded.
- With its 1,998th performance, Agatha Christie's "The Mousetrap" becomes Britain's longest-running play.
- Hit songs are "Maria" and "Love Letters in the Sand".

1958

World Events of 1958
- Charles de Gaulle is elected President of France.
- Queen Elizabeth II opens Gatwick Airport in England.
- The world's largest oil tanker, capable of carrying 1,021,000 barrels, is launched in Japan.
- The first radar speed checks are used in London.
- The Campaign for Nuclear Disarmament (CND) is founded.
- The Hovercraft is invented.
- Unemployment in the US reaches 5 million.
- In Stockholm, Dr Ake Senning implants the first internal heart pacemaker.
- Krushchev becomes the Soviet Prime Minister.
- America launches the first moon rocket.
- Prince Charles becomes the Prince of Wales.
- Britain's first motorway opens.
- Race riots flare in Notting Hill Gate, London.

Sporting Life
- Seven Manchester United footballers are killed in the Munich plane crash.
- Pakistan's cricket team visits the West Indies for the first time.
- In cricket, Australia defeats South Africa 3 tests to nil.
- The Grand National is won by Mr What.
- In football, Bolton Wanderers beat Manchester United to win the FA Cup.

The Arts
- "The Bridge on the River Kwai" wins 3 British Academy Awards.
- Boris Pasternak wins the Nobel Prize for Literature and publishes his novel "Dr Zhivago".
- Hit songs are "Magic Moments" and "All I Have to do is Dream".
- The film "Gigi" wins nine Oscars.

Above:
Margaret Thatcher, seen here with her twins Mark and Carole, became Member of Parliament for Finchley in 1959.

Above right:
Buddy Holly, with his band, The Crickets, created a sensational new sound in popular music and made a major contribution to the birth of a teen culture in the West. His songs were recorded by other artists and strongly influenced The Beatles. He died in an air crash during a punishing tour of concerts.

1959

World Events of 1959
- Britain recognises Fidel Castro as leader of a new government in Cuba.
- Rock singer Buddy Holly dies in a plane crash.
- The first section of the London-Birmingham motorway (Ml) opens.
- In France, work begins on a road tunnel beneath Mont Blanc.
- Britain and Iceland are engaged in a "Cod War".
- In the US, the state of Alabama bans a children's book because it shows a black rabbit marrying a white one.
- Cinema attendances drop in the UK as TV booms.
- In the UK, Margaret Thatcher enters parliament.
- Russia produces the first pictures of the far side of the moon.
- In the UK, the number of people going to University has doubled since 1939.
- In an international treaty, 12 countries agree to preserve the Antarctic as a science reserve.

Sporting Life
- In football, Nottingham Forest beat Luton Town 2-1 to win the FA Cup Final.
- In cricket, Australia defeats England 4 tests to nil.
- Golfer Jack Nicklaus wins the USGA Amateur title.
- In tennis, Australia wins the Davis Cup against the US.
- British racing driver Stirling Moss wins the Italian Grand Prix.

The Arts
- A work of art by Picasso is sold for £55,000, a world-record for a living artist.
- The film "Ben Hur" opens in Britain and Australia.
- Hit songs are "What do you Want to Make those Eyes at me For?" and "Livin' Doll".
- D.H. Lawrence's book "Lady Chatterley's Lover" is banned in the US.
- Actor David Niven wins an Oscar.

1960

World Events of 1960
- The actor Clark Gable dies.
- The population of the US is nearly 180 million.
- Mrs Bandaranaike becomes Prime Minister of Ceylon, the world's first woman Prime Minister.
- Australian aborigines become Australian Citizens and are eligible for Social Service benefits.
- The first weather satellite is launched by the US.
- John Fitzgerald Kennedy becomes the President of the US.
- The Congo is given its independence.
- In Britain, 200,000 copies of "Lady Chatterley's Lover" by D.H. Lawrence, sell out in one day.
- National Service ends in Britain.
- In Johannesburg, South Africa, all black political organisations are banned.
- Cyprus claims its independence from Britain.
- Women ministers are accepted for the first time by the Swedish Church.
- Leonid Brezhnev becomes Soviet President.
- The laser beam is invented.

Sporting Life
- The Olympic Games open in Rome.
- 16 year old Bobby Fischer successfully defends the US chess crown.
- In tennis, Australia defeats Spain to win the Davis Cup .
- In football, Real Madrid win the European Cup for the fifth time in a row.
- US boxers, including Cassius Clay win three gold medals in the Olympics.

The Arts
- The film "Psycho" opens.
- Hit songs are "Let's Do the Twist" and "It's a Itsy Bitsy Teeny Weeny Yellow Polka Dot Bikini".
- "Ben Hur" starring Charlton Heston wins a record 10 Oscars.

Left:
John F Kennedy was elected US President in 1960. In his inaugural address he said, "Ask not what your country can do for you - ask what can you do for your country."

- The Royal Shakespeare Company is inaugurated in Britain.

1961

World Events of 1961
- The millionth Morris Minor is produced.
- Britain applies to join the Common Market.
- The Orient Express runs from Paris to Bucharest for the last time.
- Soviet cosmonaut Yuri Gagarin becomes the first man in space.

- The Bay of Pigs in Cuba is invaded.
- Fossil bones are discovered in Africa, pushing the origins of humans back millions of years.
- The first pay-phones are installed in the UK.
- Russian ballet dancer Rudolf Nureyev defects to the west.
- The contraceptive pill goes on sale in the UK and Australia.
- John F. Kennedy is sworn in as the youngest President of the US.
- The construction of the Berlin Wall begins.
- Malta gains independence from Britain.
- In Rabat, Hassan II becomes King of Morocco, on the death of King Mohammed V.
- South Africa becomes a republic and leaves the Commonwealth.
- The earliest surviving mosaics in Britain are discovered at Fishbourne.

Sporting Life
- In tennis, Australia beats Italy 5 games to nil to win the Davis Cup.
- South African golfer Gary Player wins the US Masters by a single stroke.
- At Wimbledon, Australian Rod Laver wins the men's singles final.
- In Monaco, Stirling Moss wins the Monaco Grand Prix.

The Arts
- Marlene Dietrich stars in "Judgment at Nuremburg".
- Walt Disney's "101 Dalmations" is released.
- Hit songs are "Wooden Heart" and "You Don't Know".
- American novelist Ernest Hemingway commits suicide.
- In the UK, the Shakepeare Memorial Theatre at Stratford-on-Avon becomes the Royal Shakespeare Theatre.
- "Pop Art", a new art movement becomes popular.

Above:
On April 12 1961 the Soviet Union put the first man into space. Major Yuri Gagarin, 27, orbited the earth and made a safe return. He reportedly told the Soviet premier Kruschev, "I could see seas, mountains, big cities, rivers and forests."

Right:
The celebrated dancer Rudolf Nureyev was granted political asylum in Paris after making a dash for freedom from the Soviet 'minders' accompanying the Kirov Ballet just as they were leaving for London. He was one of the greatest ballet dancers of all time.

1962

World Events of 1962

- Marilyn Monroe dies.
- There is an outbreak of smallpox in Britain.
- John Glenn is the first American to orbit the earth.
- The world's population is more than 3 billion.
- Amnesty International is created.
- The Cuban missile crisis sees the world on the brink of a nuclear war.
- In Australia, Aborigines are granted the right to vote.
- "The Twist" is the latest dance craze.
- Jamaica, Trinidad and Tobago are granted their independence .
- French leader Charles de Gaulle survives an assassination attempt.
- In Stockholm, Sweden, two sisters who are married to two brothers, give birth in the same hospital on the same day.
- In London, share values fall by £1,000 million, the biggest slump since 1929.
- In San Francisco, three prisoners dig their way out of Alcatraz using spoons.
- In Washington, the Supreme Court bans "official prayers" in schools.

Sporting Life

- The Commonwealth games open in Perth, Australia.
- In football, Brazil win the World Cup.
- Australian tennis player Rod Laver becomes the first Australian to win the Grand Slam.
- Australia wins a record 38 Commonwealth Games gold medals.
- In Karachi, England cricketers win the Test series against Pakistan.

The Arts

- Elizabeth Taylor and Richard Burton star in "Cleopatra".
- "Pop Art" by Andy Warhol and Roy Lichtenstein is all the rage.
- "A Clockwork Orange", a novel by Anthony Burgess is published.

- The film "Lawrence of Arabia" is released.
- Hit songs are "I Remember You" and "Blowin' in the Wind".

- John Steinbeck wins the Nobel Prize for Literature.

Left:
Marilyn Monroe made 23 films and became the ultimate sex symbol. Her life was lonely and troubled and she was found dead in her bed with an empty bottle of sleeping pills on the bedside table.

1963

Left:

President Kennedy supported the Civil Rights movement, but its greatest hero was Martin Luther King. In a famous speech he said, "I have a dream that one day this nation will rise up and live out the true meaning of its creed: 'We hold these truths to be self-evident, that all men are created equal'."

World Events of 1963

- John F. Kennedy is assassinated in Dallas.
- Martin Luther King leads 200,000 in a civil rights march.
- The Profumo scandal rocks the British government.
- In Canada, archaeologists find Viking remains dating from 500 years before Columbus's arrival in America.
- Britain is refused entry into the EEC.
- Khrushchev warns that a nuclear war would kill 800 million people.
- The Americans, Soviets and British sign a nuclear test ban.

- The Great Train Robbery takes place.
- Kenya gains its independence.
- In Britain, the BBC ends its ban on mentioning royalty, politics, religion and sex in its comedy shows.
- A 50 mph speed limit is introduced in the UK, but ignored by most drivers.
- A "hot-line" between the White House and the Kremlin is introduced.
- A new island is created off the south coast of Iceland, following volcanic activity on the ocean floor.

Sporting Life

- Football team Tottenham become the first British team to win the European Cup Winners Cup.
- Athlete Bob Hayes runs 100 yards in a record 9.1 seconds.
- Margaret Smith is the first Australian woman to win Wimbledon.
- In cricket, the West Indies win the Test series against England.
- Boxer Sonny Liston successfully defends his heavyweight crown.

The Arts

- The Beatles record their first LP "Please Please Me".
- "Lawrence of Arabia" wins seven Oscars.
- Alfred Hitchcock's film "The Birds" is released.
- Hit songs are "She Loves You" and "From Me to You".
- The James Bond movie "From Russia With Love" is released.
- The film "The Great Escape" is released.

Left:

It is said that everyone alive at the time remembers exactly where they were, whom they were with and what they were doing when they heard the tragic news that Predident John F Kennedy had been shot dead in Dallas. The whole world mourned a much loved and admired President.

1964

World Events of 1964
- Harold Wilson becomes the Prime Minister of Britain.
- Beatlemania sweeps through the US.
- The United Nations sends peace-keeping force to Cyprus.
- The US bombs North Vietnam.
- In South Africa, Nelson Mandela is sentenced to life imprisonment.
- Race riots break out in Harlem, New York.
- Dr Martin Luther King is awarded the Nobel Peace Prize.
- Krushchev is ousted in USSR and Brezhnev and Kosygin rise to power.
- Topless swimsuits appear in the south of France.
- In Northern Rhodesia, Kenneth Kaunda, the nation's first premier, is sworn in.
- £10 notes are issued for the first time in the UK since World War II.
- France and Britain agree to construct a Channel Tunnel costing £160 million.
- In Jerusalem, the Palestine Liberation Organisation is created.
- Europe's longest bridge, the Forth Road Bridge, opens in the UK.

Sporting Life
- The Olympic Games are held in Tokyo.
- In British football, West Ham win the FA Cup Final.
- Boxer Cassius Clay wins the heavyweight championship of the world.
- Dawn Fraser wins her 8th Olympic medal – an Australian record.
- In cricket, Australia draw the test series with South Africa.
- South Africa is banned from the Olympics for apartheid policies.

The Arts
- Julie Andrews stars in "Mary Poppins".
- Ernest Hemingway's novel "A Moveable Feast" is published.
- Hit songs are "I Love You Because" and "It's Over".

- "The Great Escape" is released.
- "Fiddler on the Roof" opens on Broadway.
- The film "The Pink Panther" opens starring Peter Sellers.

- Sidney Poitier becomes the first black to win an Oscar, for best actor in "Lillies of the Field".
- French novelist Jean-Paul Sartre rejects a Nobel Prize.

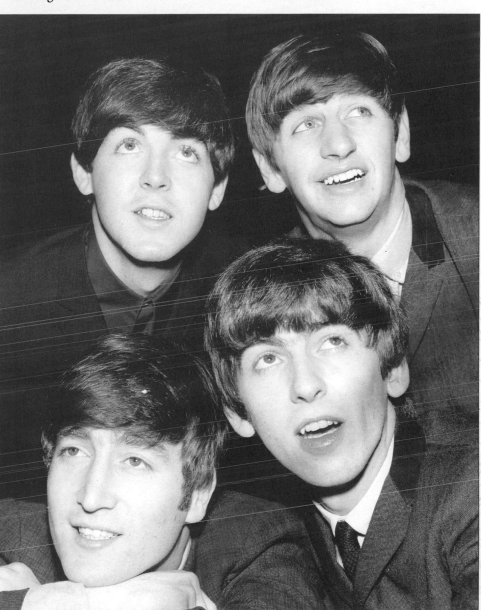

Left:
John, Paul, George and Ringo were pursued by thousands of screaming fans at airports and concerts, giving rise to a new phenomenon in pop music. The Beatles first appeared in the United States in 1964 on the Ed Sullivan Show.

1965

World Events of 1965

- American Edward White is the first astronaut to walk in space.
- Malcolm X, Black Muslim leader, is assassinated in New York.
- In Britain, the death penalty is abolished.
- Sir Winston Churchill dies.
- The Beatles are awarded MBEs.
- The first woman High Court judge, Judge Elizabeth Lane is appointed in Britain.
- The US suffers its biggest power cut in American history when New York City and parts of nine states are blacked out.
- United Nations Children's Fund (UNICEF) is awarded the Nobel Peace Prize.
- Guerrilla leader Che Guevara leaves Cuba.
- The first Japanese cars are imported to the UK.
- Lyndon B. Johnson is sworn in as the new President of the US.
- A violent cyclone in East Pakistan kills over 10,000.
- The state of New York abolishes the death sentence.

Above:
The British nation and the world mourned the century's greatest leader. Thousands queued day and night to file past Winston Churchill's bier as he lay in state in Westminster Hall, and tributes poured in from around the globe.

Left:
Gary Player winning the British Open Golf Championship.

- In the US, Yale University claims that a 1440 map proves that the Vikings discovered North America.

Sporting Life
- Gary Player wins the US Open Golf championship. Jack Nicklaus wins the Masters.
- 12 year-old South African Karen Muir swims 110 yards backstroke in a world record 68.7 seconds.
- In cricket the West Indies defeats Australia 2 tests to 1.
- In English football, Liverpool beat Leeds United to win the FA Cup Final for the first time.

- Boxer Cassius Clay beats Sonny Liston for the world title.

The Arts
- The Seekers "I'll Never Find Another You" is the first Australian record to sell one million copies.
- The Rolling Stones have three number one hits in Britain.
- "The Sound of Music" wins an Academy Award.
- Hit songs are "A Hard Day's Night" and "A Walk in the Black Forest".
- The Beatles star in the film "Help!"

1966

Left:

Mini skirts caused a furore when they first hit the fashion scene, but before long it was not only the young and beautiful who were showing a few inches of thigh. And hemlines rose a little with each passing year.

Right:

England team members carry their captain Bobby Moore shoulder high as he brandishes the World Cup.

World Events of 1966

- Floods in north Italy ruin thousands of art treasures in Florence.
- In London, Myra Hindley and Ian Brady go on trial at the Old Bailey for the "Moors Murders".
- Mao Tse-tung proclaims a Cultural Revolution in China.
- Indira Gandhi becomes Prime Minister of India.
- Britain is replaced by Japan as Australia's best trade customer.
- In America, the first black senator, Edward W. Brooke, is elected.
- Random roadside breathalysers are introduced in Britain.
- Supermarkets are becoming popular throughout Europe and the Far East.
- The Labour government declares a State of Emergency because of a seamen's strike.
- Barcelona police beat up 100 priests protesting at police brutality.
- 83 year old Eamon de Valera is re-elected President of Ireland.
- Race riots flare up in the US.

Sporting Life

- Boxer Cassius Clay beats Henry Cooper to retain the world heavyweight championship.
- England footballers beat Germany to win the World Cup 4-2.
- In tennis, Australia defeats India in the Davis Cup.
- Billie-Jean King wins the women's singles title at Wimbledon.
- In horse racing, the Cheltenham Gold Cup is won by Arkle for the third year running.

The Arts

- The Mamas and the Papas introduce soft rock.
- Hit songs are "Eleanor Rigby" and "Strangers in the Night".
- Frank Sinatra and Mia Farrow marry.
- The Beatles play their last live concert.
- Elizabeth Taylor stars in "Who's Afraid of Virgina Woolf?"
- In London, the West End's longest running musical "Oliver!" ends its run of six years, three months.

1967

World Events of 1967

- In Cape Town, the world's first human heart transplant is successfully carried out.
- British yachtsman Francis Chichester completes a solo round the world voyage.
- Israel wages a six-day war against the Arab states.
- The microwave oven is introduced in the US.
- President Lyndon Johnson visits the US troops in Vietnam.
- Britain's largest new town will occupy 22,000 acres of Buckinghamshire and be called "Milton Keynes".
- In Britain, ITV starts broadcasting "News At Ten", a daily half-hour news programme.
- The British model Twiggy hits the fashion world.
- Donald Campbell dies attempting to break the world water speed record.

- In Britain's biggest ever bullion raid, £700,000 in gold bars is stolen from a security van.
- In Nigeria, government troops invade Biafra and Europeans flee.
- In Britain, the £8 million Dartford Tunnel under the Thames opens.
- Che Guevara, Argentinian revolutionary, is shot dead.

Sporting Life

- In England 100-1 outsider Foinavov wins this year's Grand National.
- Heavyweight boxer Muhammed Ali is indicted for refusing to fight in Vietnam.
- In cricket, South Africa defeats Australia 3 test to 1 in South Africa.

- In baseball, St Louis Cardinals beat the Boston Red Sox to win the World Series.
- In Monaco, a Mini Cooper wins the Monte Carlo rally.

The Arts

- Dustin Hoffman stars in "The Graduate".
- Elizabeth Taylor wins an Oscar for "Who's Afraid of Virginia Woolf?"
- "A Man For All Seasons" wins six Oscars.
- Elivis Presley marries Priscilla Beaulieu.
- Hit songs are "Release Me" and "All You Need is Love".
- The Beatles release the "Sergeant Pepper's" album.

Below left:
After the Six Day Arab-Israeli war, the West Bank was occupied by Israel.

Below:
The Russian agent Kim Philby fled to the Soviet Union in 1963 where he eventually became a senior officer in the KGB. In 1967 he gave his first interview to British journalists.

1968

World Events of 1968
- Richard Nixon is elected President of the United States.
- In Egypt, the Aswan Dam is completed.
- The Civil rights leader Dr Martin Luther King is assassinated in Memphis.
- Russia invades Czechoslovakia.
- Anti-Vietnam demonstrations take place in London.
- French students revolt in Paris.
- Robert Kennedy is shot dead.
- Anti-government protests break out in Warsaw.
- Abortion is legalised in Britain.
- There is a wave of student riots throughout Europe following the shooting of left-wing student leader Rudi Dutschke.
- The first decimal coins come into circulation in the UK —five New Pence and ten New Pence.
- President Charles de Gaulle has a landslide victory in France's general election.
- The epidural technique, a new method of relieving pain in childbirth, is used for the first time.
- In London, the Family Law Reform Bill is published, aiming to lower the age of adulthood from 21 to 18.

Sporting Life
- Rod Laver beats fellow Australian Tony Roche to win Wimbledon.
- The Olympic Games are held in Mexico City.
- In cricket, Australia defeats India 4 tests to nil.
- English football team Manchester United win the European Cup.
- Tony Jacklin is the first English golfer to win a major US golf tournament for more than 20 years.

The Arts
- Hit songs are "Hey Jude", "Wonderful World" and "Those Were the Days".
- The musical "Hair" opens in London.
- John Updike's novel "Couples" is published.
- American novelist John Steinbeck dies
- The film "2001: A Space Odyssey" is released.

Below:
Attempts to reform the communist system in Czechoslovakia led to an invasion by the USSR and their allies who feared that reform would spread to their countries.

1969

World Events of 1969

- War breaks out between El Salvador and Honduras after a football match.
- Israel elects its first woman premier, Golda Meir.
- Inflation is a worldwide problem.
- In Britain, the voting age is reduced to 18.
- The first man, Neil Armstrong, lands on the moon.
- Yassir Arafat is appointed the new leader of the PLO.
- The Woodstock Festival in the US is attended by some 400,000 people.
- Britain is admitted into the EEC.
- British troops move into Belfast.
- The Kray twins are jailed for 30 years.
- At the age of 18, Bernadette Devlin becomes the youngest ever British MP.
- Colonel Gaddafi becomes leader of Libya.
- In New York, two university campuses are closed because of student rioting.

Sporting Life

- Manchester City beat Leicester City to win the English FA Cup Final.
- Golfer Tony Jacklin wins the British Open.
- The US tennis team retains the Davis Cup, beating the Rumanians.
- Brazilian football star Pele scores his 1000th goal.
- In cricket, Australia defeats the West Indies 3 tests to 1.

The Arts

- Frank Sinatra releases "My Way".
- Beatles star Paul McCartney marries Linda Eastman.
- Mario Puzo's book "The Godfather" is published.
- The Rolling Stones play at Madison Gardens, US.
- Hit songs are "My Way" and "Gentle on My Mind".
- Rolling Stones member Brian Jones drowns at the age of 25.
- Dennis Hopper stars in the film "Easy Rider".
- French novelist Samuel Beckett is awarded the Nobel Prize for Literature.

1970

Sporting Life
- South Africa is banned from the 1972 Olympics.
- Australia loses the Americas Cup 4 to 1.
- British golfer Tony Jacklin wins the US Open.
- Brazil wins football's World Cup.

The Arts
- John Wayne wins an Oscar for "True Grit".
- Janis Joplin dies.
- The film M*A*S*H wins first prize at the Cannes Film Festival.
- Hit songs are "Yellow River", "The Wonder of You" and "In the Summertime".
- Guitarist Jimi Hendrix dies at the age of 28.
- Bernice Rubens wins the Booker Prize for her novel "The Elected Member."

Below:
The genius of composer and rock guitarist Jimi Hendrix was cut short by his tragic death on September 18 1970. His unique sound has inspired many of today's great rock musicians.

World Events of 1970
- Edward Heath becomes British Prime Minister.
- The Beatles officially split.
- The "Hong Kong" flu kills 2,850 people in Britain in one week.
- US troops are sent to Cambodia.
- Violence erupts at the Suez Canal.
- Arab terrorists hijack five aeroplanes and explode three.
- Charles de Gaulle dies in France.
- In Britain, the age of voting is reduced from 21 to 18.
- In Ceylon, Mrs Bandaranaike is re-elected Prime Minister.
- Cambodia is declared a republic.

1971

World Events of 1971
- Britain converts to decimal currency.
- Riots break out in Ulster, Northern Ireland.
- Two American astronauts go for a drive on the moon.
- The bombing of North Vietnam continues.
- Bangladesh becomes independent.
- China joins the UN, against the protests of US and Taiwan.
- Idi Amin becomes dictator in Uganda.
- On the French Riviera, hundreds of women are ordered to put their bikini tops back on.
- Britain expels 90 Russians for spying.
- Mount Etna erupts.
- In the UK, the first divorce is granted under the Divorce Act.

Sporting Life
- British boxer Henry Cooper retires from the ring.
- The Australian tennis player Evonne Goolagong wins Wimbledon.
- British golfers win the Walker Cup for the first time since 1938.

The Arts
- Glenda Jackson stars in "Women in Love".
- Sylvia Plath's novel "The Bell Jar" is published posthumously.
- Hit songs are "Chirpy, Chirpy, Cheep, Cheep" and "Maggie May".
- Anthony Burgess' novel "A Clockwork Orange" is made into a film.
- "Love Story" by Eric Segal is published.

Right:
The Lunar Rover, the first manned surface vehicle was transported to the moon by Apollo 15. Many experiments were carried out on the moon's surface, and 77 kg of soil and rocks were brought back to earth to be analysed.

1972

World Events of 1972
- The Queen Elizabeth liner is destroyed by fire in Hong Kong.
- Arab terrorists massacre 11 Israeli athletes at the Munich Olympics.
- Miners strike in Britain.
- Violence increases in Northern Ireland, leading to the "Bloody Sunday" killings in Ulster.
- Apollo 17 makes its longest and final visit to the moon.
- 10,000 people die in an earthquake in Nicaragua.
- West Germany signs non-aggression pacts with the Soviet Union and Poland.
- Britain signs the EEC treaty.
- Richard Nixon is re-elected President of the US.

Sporting Life
- Stan Smith wins Wimbledon's men's singles final.
- American swimmer Mark Spitz wins a record 7 gold medals in the Olympics.
- Russian gymnast Olga Korbut wins three gold medals at the Olympics.

The Arts
- Liza Minnelli stars in "Cabaret".
- King Tutankhamun's treasures are exhibited in Britain.
- Hit songs are "Amazing Grace" and "Puppy Love".
- Marlon Brando stars in the film "The Godfather".
- Alfred Hitchcock directs the film "Frenzy".
- Richard Adams' "Watership Down" is published.
- In London, John Betjeman is appointed Poet Laureate.

Below left:
11 Israeli athletes were massacred by Palestinian terrorists in Munich.

Below:
Pedal-power in Italy during the fuel crisis.

1973

World Events of 1973
- Princess Anne and Captain Mark Phillips marry at Westminster Abbey.
- Crown Prince Carl Gustaf becomes King of Sweden.
- There is a ceasefire in Vietnam.
- The Watergate scandal breaks in Washington.
- Yom Kippur war erupts between Israel and Egypt.
- In Athens, Greece is declared a Republic.
- John Paul Getty III is kidnapped.
- The World Trade Center is completed in New York.
- Britain, Denmark and Ireland join the EEC.
- VAT is introduced in the UK.
- East and West Germany establish diplomatic relations.

Sporting Life
- Star tennis players boycott Wimbledon.
- Ajax Amsterdam win football's European Cup for the third year running.
- The Grand National is won in a record time of nine minutes 1.9 seconds by Red Rum.

The Arts
- Artist Pablo Picasso dies at the age of 91.
- The film "Jesus Christ Superstar" is released.
- Robert Redford and Paul Newman star in "The Sting".
- Erica Jong's book "Fear of Flying" is published.
- Hit songs are "Tie a Yellow Ribbon" and "Blockbuster".
- "The Exorcist" is released.

1974

World Events of 1974
- Britain's first McDonald's restaurant opens in London.
- Cyclone Fifi in Honduras kills 10,000 people.
- President Nixon is the first US President to resign from power, and is succeeded by Gerald Ford.
- Heiress Patty Hearst is kidnapped in California.
- French President Georges Pompidou dies and is succeeded by Giscard d'Estaing.
- Lord Lucan is sought in Britain and Europe for the murder of his nanny, and an attack on his estranged wife.
- Prince Juan Carlos takes over from Franco in Spain.
- Turkey invades Cyprus.
- In Australia, a cyclone hits Darwin.

Sporting Life
- West Germany win football's World Cup.
- Tennis couple Jimmy Connors and Chris Evert both win their respective Wimbledon singles titles.

The Arts
- Ballet dancer Mikhail Baryshnikov defects from Russia.
- Hit songs are "Seasons in the Sun" and "The Way We Were".
- Robert Redford stars in "The Great Gatsby".
- John Le Carre's book "Tinker, Tailor, Soldier, Spy" is published.
- Abba win the Eurovision Song Contest with "Waterloo".
- Jack Nicholson stars in "Chinatown".

Right:
Richard Nixon resigned as President of the United States when it was revealed that he was implicated in the Watergate scandal, in which White House officials had obstructed investigations into a burglary at the Democratic Party headquarters.

1975

World Events of 1975
- The Suez Canal re-opens after 8 years.
- The monarchy returns to Spain with Juan Carlos becoming King.
- A terracotta army of 6,000 life-sized soldiers dating from the 3rd century BC is discovered in China.
- The last US troops leave Saigon.
- In Hawaii, Mauna Loa volcano erupts.
- The Channel Tunnel is abandoned by the British Government.
- The Khmer Rouge overrun Cambodia.
- Over 6.5 million elm trees are killed by Dutch elm disease in England.
- Margaret Thatcher becomes the first woman leader of a British political party.

Sporting Life
- Czechoslovakian tennis player Martina Navratilova defects to the US.
- The West Indies win cricket's first World Cup.
- At 23, Anatoly Karpov becomes the world's young-est chess champion.
- Arthur Ashe is the first black men's singles champion at Wimbledon.

The Arts
- Hit songs are "Bohemian Rhapsody" and "Sailing".
- "One Flew Over the Cuckoo's Nest" starring Jack Nicholson wins 5 Oscars.
- John Cleese appears in the English television series "Fawlty Towers" for the first time.
- Steven Spielberg's film "Jaws" is released.

Right:
The United States government had maintained a military presence in South East Asia since 1946 with the intention of preventing communism spreading in the region. 50,000 Americans lost their lives in the disastrous Vietnam War.

1976

World Events of 1976
- Britain's new Prime Minister is James Callaghan.
- Concorde makes its first commercial flights.
- Racial violence erupts in South Africa.
- Britain suffers its worst drought in 250 years.
- American spacecraft Viking I lands on Mars.
- Jimmy Carter is elected President of the US.
- The world's most violent earthquake for 12 years hits China.
- In Uganda, Israeli commandoes rescue 105 hos-tages at Entebbe Airport.

- The Queen opens Birmingham's £45 million National Exhibition Centre.
- The Seychelles islands become independent after 162 years of British rule.

Sporting Life
- Austrian racing driver Niki Lauda is seriously injured in an accident in the German Grand Prix.
- Rumanian gymnast Nadia Comaneci is awarded the first maximum score of 10.00 at the Olympics in Montreal.

The Arts
- Hit songs are "Save Your Kisses for Me", "Mississippi" and "Don't Go Breaking My Heart".
- Sylvester Stallone stars in the film "Rocky".
- The film "Taxi Driver" is released starring Robert de Niro.
- The Tate Gallery causes a stir when it exhibits "Low Sculpture"—120 bricks laid in oblong.

Right:
Idi Amin was President of Uganda from 1971 until 1979, during which time around 300,000 Uganda were murdered. He is known to have personally ordered the deaths of his political opponents.

Left:
Fans and admirers all over the world were shocked to hear of the death of Elvis Presley at the age of 42.

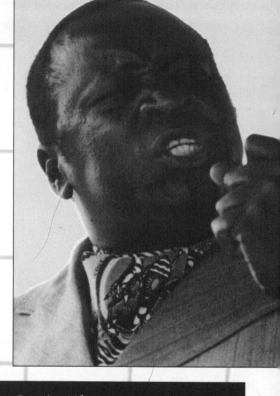

1977

World Events of 1977
- Queen Elizabeth II celebrates her Silver Jubilee.
- Refugees flee from Vietnam.
- In South Africa, black rights leader Steve Biko dies in detention.
- Spain holds its first democratic election for 41 years.
- Uganda's Idi Amin holds 240 Americans hostage.
- Gary Gilmore is the first convict to be executed in the US for ten years.
- The average price for a house in London is £16,731.
- The Spanish government requests entry into the EEC.
- President Anwar Sadat becomes the first Arab leader to visit Israel.

Sporting Life
- Red Rum wins his third Grand National at Liverpool, England.
- Nigel Short, England's chess prodigy, qualifies for a national chess final at the age of 11.
- In football, Liverpool win the League for a record tenth time.

The Arts
- The Pompidou Centre for the Arts opens in Paris.
- Hit songs are "When I Need You" and "Don't Cry for Me, Argentina".
- The film "Star Wars" takes a record $185 million at the box office.
- Woody Allen stars in "Annie Hall". The film "Close Encounters of the Third Kind" is released.

World Events of 1978

- A Polish cardinal becomes the Catholic Church's first ever non-Italian Pope since 1542.
- The world's first air balloon crossing of the Atlantic is made.
- The world's first test tube baby, Louise Brown, is born in Manchester.
- Sweden becomes the first country to pass a law against aerosol sprays which affect the ozone layer.
- South African journalist Donald Woods escapes to Lesotho.
- Pieter Willem Botha is elected the new Prime Minister of South Africa.
- US President Jimmy Carter brings Egypt's Anwar Sadat and Israel's Menachem Begin together at Camp David.

Sporting Life

- The Ryder Cup is opened to European golfers, after more than 50 years as a match between the US and Great Britain.
- Argentina wins football's World Cup.

The Arts

- The film "Superman" is released.
- John Travolta and Oliver Newton-John star in the film "Grease".
- Hit songs are "Rivers of Babylon" and "Summer Nights".
- Robert de Niro stars in the film "The Deer Hunter".
- Andrew Lloyd Webber and Tim Rice's opera-musical "Evita" is a hit.

Left:

Polish born Pope John Paul II is a champion for peace, justice, and human rights in the world and has won the respect of political leaders of all religious faiths. He was seriously injured in an attempted assassination in St. Peter's Square in 1981 and later visited his attacker, Mehmet Ali Agca, in prison to assure him of his forgiveness.

1979

Below right:

Below right:
Ayatollah Khomeni, the Islamic fundamentalist was exiled to France in 1973 where he led a movement against the Shah of Iran. When the Shah left, Khomeni returned to lead the country.

Below:
The Afghan Marxist government requested the help of the USSR whose armies occupied the country in 1979. The ensuing war had little popular support in the USSR was a major contribution to the collapse of the Soviet Union in 1991.

World Events of 1979
- Voyager I discovers rings around Jupiter.
- Israel and Egypt sign a peace treaty.
- Margaret Thatcher is elected Britain's first woman Prime Minister.
- The Sony Walkman comes on the market.
- The Rubik's Cube goes on sale in the US.
- Mother Teresa is awarded the Nobel Peace Prize.
- Ayatollah Khomeini returns to Iran.
- The Soviet Union invades Afghanistan.
- Pope John Paul II visits the US.
- Rhodesia is renamed Zimbabwe.
- US President Jimmy Carter and Leonard Brezhnev sign the SALT Treaty.

Sporting Life
- Spanish golfer Severiano Ballesteros wins the British Open.
- Trevor Francis becomes Britain's first million-pound footballer.
- British athlete Sebastian Coe breaks three world records (800 metre, 1,500 metres and the mile).

The Arts
- Films released this year include Francis Ford Coppola's "Apocalypse Now", starring Martin Sheen and Marlon Brando.
- Hit songs are "Heart of Glass" and "Bright Eyes".
- Woody Allen stars in "Manhattan".
- "Kramer vs. Kramer" is released, starring Meryl Streep & Dustin Hoffman.

Below inset panel:
The Solidarity Labour Movement in Poland, which fought for democratic reforms in the early 1980s, was led by Lech Walesa. He was imprisoned by the communist authorities in 1982, and won the Nobel Peace Prize in 1983.

Right & opposite page:
Soldiers in Egyptian President Anwar Sadat's stopped their vehicles in the middle of a parade and opened fire on the president and his party. He was killed along with five others.

1980

World Events of 1980
- Sanjay Gandhi, son of India's Prime Minister, dies in a plane crash.
- Mount St Helens erupts in the United States.
- The SAS rescues 19 hostages from the Iranian embassy in London.
- Two years of drought bring famine to East Africa.
- Former Hollywood actor Ronald Reagan is elected President of the USA.
- 3,000 die in Italian earthquake.

1981

- The US boycott the Olympic Games in Moscow in protest against the Soviet Union's invasion of Afghanistan.
- Voyager 1 sends pictures of Saturn to earth.
- Margaret Thatcher declares she is 'not for turning'.
- The wreck of the "Titanic" is located.

Sporting Life
- British athletes Sebastian Coe and Steve Ovett win Olympic gold medals.
- Bjorn Borg wins Wimbledon for the fifth time.
- Welsh boxer Johnny Owen dies after a title fight against Mexico's Lupe Pintor.

The Arts
- Steve McQueen loses his battle against cancer.
- John Lennon is shot dead.
- John Hurt plays "The Elephant Man".
- Britain apologises to Saudi Arabia for the TV programme, "Death of a Princess."
- British TV audiences are hooked on "Dallas".

World Events of 1981
- The Prince of Wales marries Lady Diana Spencer.
- In China, Mao Tse-tung's widow is condemned for her part in the Cultural Revolution.
- An attempt is made to assassinate President Reagan.
- Race riots hit many towns in Britain.
- Martial law is imposed in Poland following strikes and demonstrations.
- The first cases of AIDS among homosexuals and drug users are identified in American cities.
- The guillotine is abolished in France.
- The stock market suffers the second worst fall in its history.
- IRA hunger striker, Bobby Sands is elected an MP but dies a few weeks later, provoking riots.

Sporting Life
- Torville and Dean become European ice dancing champions.
- Bob Champion, who was diagnosed with cancer and given 8 months to live Grand National.
- England wins the test series 3-1 against Australia.
- Steve Davis wins the world snooker championships.

The Arts
- "Brideshead Revisited" is serialised on British television.
- "Cats", a ballet-musical by Andrew Lloyd Webber, hits the London stage.
- "Chariots Of Fire" and "The French Lieutenant"s Woman" were released.
- Hit songs are "Stand and Deliver" and "Imagine".

Below:

Millions around the world watched on TV as the Prince of Wales and Lady Diana Spencer made their vows in St. Paul's Cathedral. The crowds that gathered around Buckingham Palace were treated to the customary appearance of the couple on the balcony, and a memorable and very public embrace.

1982

World Events of 1982

- Mark Thatcher, son of the British Prime Minister goes missing in the Sahara Desert.
- Unemployment in Britain is above 3 million.
- Britain goes to war with Argentina over the Falkland Islands.
- The Princess of Wales gives birth to her first son, Prince William.
- Henry VIII's flagship, the Mary Rose, which sank in the Solent in 1545 with great loss of life, is raised from the sea-bed.
- Princess Grace of Monaco, formally actress Grace Kelly, dies in a car crash.
- Peace keeping troops from the USA, France and Italy are sent to Beirut. British troops join them later.
- Spain gives up its claim to Gibraltar.
- The first test-tube twins are born in Cambridge.
- Sophia Loren goes to jail for tax evasion.

Sporting Life

- Tom Watson became the fifth man to win both the British and US Open Golf Championships in the same year.
- Italy wins the World Cup, beating West Germany 3-1 in Madrid.
- Ian Botham achieves his highest Test score of 208 against India.
- Martina Navratilova and Jimmy Connors are Wimbledon champions.

The Arts

- Mrs Mary Whitehouse fails in her attempt to bring a private prosecution against Michael Bogdanov for a scene in the National Theatre play "The Romans in Britain."
- Channel Four goes on the air.
- Jacques Tati of M Hulot fame dies.
- Henry Fonda dies just 2 weeks after winning his first Oscar.

Far right:
During the 1970's 80s and 90s a campaign of terror and assassination was operated by the Provisional IRA and there were attempts on British subjects lives in Northern Ireland, the British mainland and in other countries. In October 1984 they tried to kill Margaret Thatcher and members of her Cabinet with a 20lb bomb planted in the Grand Hotel in Brighton where most of them were staying. The Prime Minister had a narrow escape. Four people died and many were injured.

Left:
More than 250 British and 650 Argentines were killed in the conflict over the Falkland Islands. Argentina has never renounced their claim to sovereignty over the territory.

1983

World Events of 1983
- Attempts are made to divert the flow of lava from the active Mount Etna.
- British voters re-elect Margaret Thatcher in a landslide victory for the Tory party.
- Cecil Parkinson is forced to resign over his affair with Sarah Keays.
- 134 IRA prisoners break out of the Maze prison.
- Gold bars worth £25 million were stolen from the Brinks-Mat warehouse at Heathrow.
- In the US, Martin Luther King's birthday is declared a national holiday.
- Polish Solidarity leader Lech Walesa is awarded the Nobel Prize for Peace.
- The Walton Sextuplets, all girls, are born in Liverpool.
- A car bomb in Beirut destroys the US embassy.
- Compact discs go on sale.

Sporting Life
- Bjorn Borg retires from tennis at the age of 26.

- Geoff Boycott is sacked by Yorkshire Cricket Club.
- In yachting, Australia wins the America's Cup.
- England beat Luxembourg 4-0, but fail to qualify for the European finals.

The Arts
- A symphony by Mozart, composed when he was 9 is discovered in Denmark.
- The British composer, Sir William Walton, dies.
- "Ghandi", a British film directed by Richard Attenborough, wins eight Oscars.
- "Every breath you take" by Police, was a hit.

Below:
The Prince and Princess of Wales with their first son, Prince William.

1984

World Events of 1984
- An astronaut takes the first untethered space walk from the US space shuttle Challenger.
- The USSR and all Eastern European countries except Romania, boycott the Los Angeles Olympic Games.
- The BMX (bicycle motorcross) craze hits Britain.
- An IRA bomb devastates the Grand Hotel in Brighton where the Tories have gathered for their annual conference.
- "Baby Fae" is given a baboon's heart in an attempt to save her life.
- Desmond Tutu is given the Nobel Peace Prize.
- Ronald Reagan is re-elected to a second term as US President.
- The scale of the Ethiopian famine is exposed by TV journalist Michael Buerk.
- Indira Gandhi is assassinated by her Sikh bodyguards.

Sporting Life
- Mary Decker trips over Zola Budd's heel in the 3000 metres Olympic final.
- Carl Lewis wins four gold medals in Los Angeles.
- John McEnroe beats Jimmy Connors to win the men's singles final at Wimbledon.
- Martina Navratilova takes the women's title for the fifth time - and her third in succession.

The Arts
- Actor Richard Burton dies.
- "Do they know it's Christmas?" tops the charts and raises millions for the starving.
- Michael Jackson's "Thriller" topped 37 million in sales.

1985

World Events of 1985
- Terry Waite frees four British hostages in Libya.
- The "Baby Cotton" surrogacy case is settled in the High Court.
- Mikhail Gorbachev becomes the new Soviet leader.
- Bangladesh is battered by a cyclone and tidal wave.
- 41 die as British football hooligans riot in Heysel, Belgium.
- Clive Sinclair unveils his C5, saying that by 2000, the petrol-powered engine will be a thing of the past.

- The pound fell to its lowest value ever - close to $1.
- 13 year old Ruth Lawrence wins a first class honours degree in Maths at Oxford.
- BBC journalists strike. The World Service is silent for one day.
- French secret agents sink the Greenpeace ship Rainbow Warrior.
- Only 1 in 3 Britons now smokes.

Sporting Life
- Tony Jacklin wins the Ryder cup.
- Zola Budd sets a new world record of 48.07 seconds in the 5,000 metres.
- Manchester United win the English FA Cup Final.
- 17 year old unseeded Boris Becker wins Wimbledon.

The Arts
- "Live Aid" raises £40 million.
- "Like a virgin" is a hit for Madonna.
- Poets Robert Graves and Philip Larkin die.
- "Les Miserables" is a stage hit.

Below:
Bob Geldof was so moved by the plight of refugees in Ethiopia that he organised the Live Aid concert to raise money to feed the starving.

1986

Left:
Prince Andrew, the Queen's second son, married Sarah Ferguson on 23 July 1986. They were given the titles Duke and Duchess of York.

World Events of 1986
- US space shuttle explodes on take-off.
- Plans for a channel tunnel are announced.
- Corazon Aquino becomes President of the Philippines.
- The Duchess of Windsor, formerly Mrs Simpson, dies.
- A nuclear reactor explodes at Chernobyl.
- Soviet dissident Andrei Sakharov is freed.
- Harold Macmillan ("Supermac") dies aged 92.
- Irish people vote against divorce.

- Prince Andrew marries Sarah Ferguson.
- The Queen and the Duke of Edinburgh visit China.
- Prince Charles admits on TV that he talks to his plants.
- Divers discover the cause of the Titanic disaster in 1912.

Sporting Life
- Mike Tyson becomes the youngest to win the WBC world heavyweight title.
- Richard Branson crosses the Atlantic in record time in Virgin Atlantic Challenger II.

- English cricketer Ian Botham admits smoking cannabis and gets a 2 month ban.
- Joe Johnson wins the Embassy World Snooker Championship as a 150-1 outsider.

The Arts
- Nigerian writer Wole Soyinka wins the Nobel Prize for Literature.
- Sculptor Henry Moore dies.
- Pop singer Boy George is convicted of possessing heroin.

Right:
The car ferry, Herald of Free Enterprise began to list and keeled over, coming to rest on a sandbank, shortly after leaving the port of Zeebrugge. An enquiry concluded that the accident was due to water flooding the car deck after the bow doors had been left open.

World Events of 1987
- Terry Waite is kidnapped in Beirut.
- Gorbachev announces reforms - perestroika (reconstruction) and glasnost (openness).
- Weathermen fail to forecast a hurricane which leaves a trail of destruction across southern England.
- The Church of England's General Synod votes in favour of the ordination of women.
- Mrs Thatcher is elected for a third term.
- Los Angeles is rocked by an earthquake.
- More than 70 nations have agreed on measures to reduce the ozone layer.
- The Herald of Free Enterprise sinks off Zeebrugge.
- The Duchess of Windsor's jewellry fetches £31m at auction.

Sporting Life
- Irish cyclist Steven Roche wins the Tour de France.
- Ben Johnson sets a new world record of 9.83 seconds in the 100 metres.
- Tottenham Hotspur's own goal gives Coventry a 3-2 win in the FA Cup.
- Nigel Mansell wins the British Grand Prix.

The Arts
- Andy Warhol dies.
- Enid Blyton's "Noddy" stories are to be revised to make them politically correct.
- "Crocodile Dundee" is a box office hit.
- Mary Whitehouse attacks the soap "Eastenders".
- One of Mozart's notebooks fetches £2.3 million at auction.

1988

World Events of 1988

- The Prince of Wales escapes death when an avalanche in Switzerland killed one of his friends.
- Artificial snow is needed to stage the Winter Olympics in Calgary.
- New licensing laws allow all day opening for British pubs.
- The Anglican Church in America appoints its first woman bishop.
- George Bush becomes US President.
- "A Brief History of Time" by Dr Stephen Hawking is a best seller.
- Benazir Bhutto becomes Prime Minister of Pakistan.
- The Chilean dictator General Pinochet is defeated in elections.
- Pan Am flight 103 explodes and crashes on Lockerbie.
- Signal failure causes a rail disaster just outside Clapham Junction.

Sporting Life

- Fourth division Wimbledon win the English football FA Cup.
- Steffi Graf wins the "Grand Slam" and an Olympic gold medal.
- Nine athletes are disqualified from the Seoul Olympics after failing drugs tests.
- Florence Griffith-Joyner wins gold medals in the 100m and 200m.

The Arts

- Michael Jackson does a concert tour of the UK.
- Prince Charles attacks modern architects English on TV.
- David Hockney staged a retrospective at the Tate in London.
- "Acrobat and Young Harlequin" by Picasso sells for £20.9 million.
- Top films are "Fatal Attraction" and "A Fish Called Wanda".

Left:
At the Olympic Games in Seoul, South Korea, the Canadian sprinter Ben Johnson was stripped of his gold medal when a routine drugs test proved positive.

1989

World Events of 1989
- Ayatollah Khomeini orders the execution of British author Salman Rushdie.
- 95 football supporters, most from Liverpool die in the Hillsborough disaster.
- Chinese government troops open fire on demonstrators in Tiananmen Square.
- The Guildford Four were freed by the appeal court after they had served 14 years for a crime they did not commit.
- An earthquake causes massive destruction in San Francisco.
- Hungary becomes a republic and free elections are promised.
- The Berlin Wall opens at the Brandenburg Gate.
- Democratic revolution frees Czechoslovakia from communist rule.
- US and Soviet leaders declare an end to the Cold War.
- 10 days of civil war in Rumania end with the capture and execution of President Ceausescu and his wife.
- Proceedings in the House of Commons are televised for the first time.

Sporting Life
- Frank Bruno fails in his attempt to take the world heavyweight title from Mike Tyson.
- Desert Orchid wins the Cheltenham Gold Cup.
- The jockey Peter Scudamore wins a record 200 races in one season.

The Arts
- Sean Connery stars with Harrison Ford in the new "Indiana Jones" film.
- Remains of Shakespeare's Globe Theatre are found.
- Kenneth Branagh directs and stars in "Henry V".

Right:
Nations within the Soviet bloc were moving towards democracy and in China students and workers were demonstrating against corruption and for political reforms. Over 1 million gathered each day in Tianenman Square. Deng Xiaoping ordered a crackdown, and possibly 1,000 people were killed.

1990

World Events of 1990
- Nelson Mandela is freed from prison.
- A protest march against the Poll Tax in London turns into a riot.
- France bans British beef imports amid concern over BSE.
- 2 English teenage girls are arrested in Bangkok in possession of heroin.
- Irish hostage Brian Keenan is released from Beirut.
- Saddam Hussein invades Kuwait and detains hundreds of foreigners in Baghdad.
- Lech Walesa wins a victory in presidential elections in Poland.
- John Major ousts Margaret Thatcher in party election to become Prime Minister.
- French and English tunnellers meet under the Channel.
- Benazir Bhutto is sacked as Prime Minister of Pakistan.

Sporting Life
- Martina Navratilova wins a record ninth ladies singles title at Wimbledon.
- West Germany wins football's World Cup in Rome.
- Stephen Hendry becomes the youngest ever world snooker champion.

The Arts
- The opera highlight is the Three Tenors at the World Cup in Rome.
- Financial problems close the Barbican and the Royal Opera House.
- "Ghost" and "Cyrano de Bergerac" are hit films.

Above:
In South Africa Nelson Mandela was sentenced to life imprisonment in 1964 for his anti government activities. After his release in February 1990 he became leader of the ANC and negotiated a peaceful transition to multiracial democracy.

1991

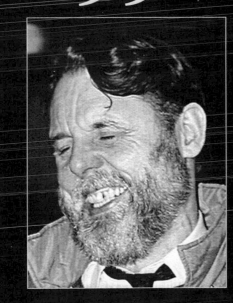

Right:
Hostage Terry Waite, on his release from captivity.

World Events of 1991
- Operation "Desert Storm" against Iraq begins.
- Saddam Hussein releases oil into the Gulf.
- The Gulf War ends after 6 weeks.
- The "Birmingham Six" are freed by an appeal court.
- Rajiv Gandhi is killed.
- Helen Sharman is Britain's first astronaut.
- Winnie Mandela is sentenced to six years in prison.
- Gorbachev collects the Nobel peace prize, and is toppled by communists.
- John McCarthy and later Terry Waite are released from captivity in Lebanon.
- A mortar lands in the garden of 10 Downing Street.
- The poll tax is abandoned.
- A new famine hits Africa.
- Yugoslavia drifts towards civil war.
- The Maxwell empire collapses after his mysterious death.

Sporting Life
- England's rugby union team wins the Five Nations championship.
- South Africa admitted to international sport after a 21 year boycott campaign.
- US athlete Mike Powell breaks the long jump record at the world championships.
- Manchester United win the European Cup-Winners Cup.

The Arts
- Pavarotti sings at a free concert in Hyde Park.
- "I do it for you" by Bryan Adams tops the UK charts for a record 16 weeks.
- On English television, David Jason stars in "The Darling Buds of May".
- Mozart features heavily in his bicentennial year.
- "Silence of the Lambs" wins five Oscars.

1992

World Events of 1992
- The West sends food and medical aid to Russia.
- The Yugoslav confederation is broken up.
- The UK suffers it's worst drought since 1745.
- Mike Tyson gets a 6 year jail sentence for rape.
- Andrew Morton publishes "Diana: Her True Story".
- The Bishop of Galway resigns after revelations that he has an illegitimate son.
- Anti-Mafia judge Falcone is murdered in Sicily.
- 58 die in race riots in Los Angeles.
- The Duchess of York announces that she is seeking a divorce, and the Prince and Princess of Wales separate.
- Windsor Castle is badly damaged by fire.
- Chris Patten becomes the last Governor of Hong Kong.

Sporting Life
- Pakistan beat England by 22 runs to win the World Cup in Melbourne.
- David Platt is sold to Italian club Juventus for £8 million.
- Nigel Mansell becomes the Formula One world champion.
- The "Unified Team" of former Soviet Union athletes scooped 112 Olympic medals.

The Arts
- Kenneth Branagh played "Hamlet".
- Paul McCartney's "Oratorio" was premiered.
- Emma Thompson wins an Oscar for her role in "Howard's End".

Right and above right:
Queen Elizabeth celebrated her 40th anniversary as sovereign but the media attention surrounding her children's marriage difficulties, added to the disaster of the fire at Windsor Castle made 1992 her "annus horibilus".

1993

World Events of 1993

- Two ten year olds are charged with the murder of James Bulger.
- The Queen volunteers to pay tax on her private income.
- Bill Clinton becomes President of the USA.
- Yitzhak Rabin and Yassir Arafat shake hands on the White House lawn.
- Former Philippines first lady Imelda Marcos is sentenced to 18 years in prison for corruption.
- Benazir Bhutto returns to power in Pakistan.
- President Yeltsin crushes a rebellion in Moscow.
- Australia restores lands to the Aborigines.
- Ffyona Campbell completes a 10,000 mile walk across Africa.
- Stella Rimington, head of MI5, reveals details of the work of her organisation.

Sporting Life

- Demonstrations bring chaos to the Grand National.
- Tennis star Monica Seles is stabbed during a match.
- Pete Sampras wins the Wimbledon men's singles championship.
- Brazil's Ayrton Senna wins the last Formula One race of the season in Adelaide.

The Arts

- Eric Clapton wins six Grammy awards.
- Top film stars call for an end to screen violence.
- Spielberg's "Jurassic Park" cost a reported £68 million to make.
- Rachel Whiteread wins the Turner prize for "Untitled Room".
- Salman Rushdie wins the 'Booker of Bookers' prize for "Midnight's Children".

Above:
Still under the sentence of death ordered by the Moslem Iranian leader Ayatollah Khomeni for the crime of blasphemy in 1989, Salman Rushdie presents his prizewinning novel, "Midnight's Children".

Left:
"Untitled Room" by Rachel Whiteread - a giant-sized sculpture in a London Street.

1994

World Events of 1994
- A major earthquake hits Los Angeles.
- Lieutenant -General Sir Michael Rose is appointed to lead a UN peacekeeping force in Bosnia.
- Priests and bishops leave the Church of England in protest at womens' ordination.
- Frederick and Rosemary West are charged with murder when 8 bodies are discovered buried at their home in Gloucester.
- Tony Blair is elected leader of the Labour Party after John Smith's death in May.
- O. J. Simpson is arrested.
- The terrorist, Carlos the Jackal, is finally captured.
- The ferry Estonia with over 1,000 passengers on board sinks in the Baltic.
- Veterans mark the 50th anniversary of the D-Day landings.
- An estimated 100,000 are killed in tribal slaughter in Rwanda.

Sporting Life
- Ayrton Senna dies in a crash at the San Marino Grand Prix.
- Brazil wins the World Cup for the fourth time.
- Torville and Dean win the British Ice Dancing championship scoring nine sixes.
- Spanish cyclist Miguel Indurain wins the Tour de France.
- Diane Modahl gets a four year ban after failing drug tests.

The Arts
- "Four Weddings and a Funeral" is a hit film.
- Steven Spielberg's "Schindler's List" wins 7 Oscars.
- The "Three Graces" sculpture by Canova is to remain in Britain.

Below:
The British Labour Party in opposition in 1994 elected Tony Blair as their new leader. Labour went on to win a landslide victory against the Conservatives in May 1997.

Left:
Veterans of the Second World War gathered on the beaches of Normandy to mark the 50th anniversary of the D-Day landings.

1995

Above:
Orphans of the war in Bosnia are treated to a visit from Santa Claus organised by international Charity Peace 2000. He brought half a million gifts donated by children in Europe.

World Events of 1995
- Kobe, a city in Japan, is devastated by an earthquake.
- Michael Foale becomes the first Briton to walk in space.
- Nick Leeson bankrupts Barings Bank.
- A religious sect is responsible for a gas attack on the Tokyo underground system.
- Sinn Fein leader Gerry Adams is welcomed at a White House party.
- Timothy McVeigh bombs the Oklahoma City's federal building.
- The first DNA database opens in Birmingham.
- Winnie Mandela is dismissed from the South African government.
- A UN women's conference is held in Beijing.
- Japan apologises for their actions during the Pacific War on the 50th anniversary of it's ending.
- O. J. Simpson is acquitted.
- The world population is 5.7 billion.

Sporting Life
- 40-1 outsider Royal Athlete wins the Grand National.
- South Africa wins the Rugby Union World Cup.
- Steffi Graf wins Wimbledon, the US Open and the French Open.

The Arts
- Rock band "Blur" wins four Brit Awards.
- Oscar Wilde is admitted to Poets' Corner in Westminster Abbey.
- "Braveheart" wins the Oscar for best film.

1996

World Events of 1996

- Hillary Clinton testifies before a grand jury investigating the Whitewater affair.
- French ex-President Francois Mitterand dies after a long illness.
- Diana agrees to Prince Charles request for a divorce.
- A teacher and 16 children are killed by a gunman at Dunblane.
- British beef exports are banned because of fears of "mad cow disease".
- Kevin and Ian Maxwell are cleared of charges of defrauding the Maxwell empire's pension funds.
- Yeltsin becomes President of Russia.
- NASA scientists say they have found evidence of possible life on Mars.
- A bomb explodes during the Olympic Games in Atlanta.
- Russian troops with draw from Chechenya.
- Taleban militia in Afghanistan capture Kabul.

Sporting Life

- England wins the Rugby Union Five Nations trophy.
- Carl Lewis takes the Olympic gold medal for long jump for the fourth time running.
- Bjarne Riis of Denmark wins the Tour de France.
- Krajicek wins the first Wimbledon men's final to be played between two unseeded players.
- Donovan Bailey sets a world record of 9.84 secs for the 100 metres.

The Arts

- "The English Patient" wins an Oscar for best film.
- Oasis dominates the British pop scene.
- The Scottish film "Trainspotting" is a surprise hit in the USA and Britain.
- The Lyric Opera of Chicago stages Wagner's "The Ring" in a performance lasting 15 hours.

Below:
Beef cattle in the U.K. were slaughtered and incinerated when it was discovered that BSE in cattle had spread to humans. The disease was spread as a result of feeding infected animal products to cattle.

Right:
Prior to their separation in 1992 the tension between the royal couple was self evident.

1997

Above & right:
Princess Diana and Mother Teresa of Calcutta captured hearts around the world.
They died within days of each other.

World Events of 1997
- Dolly the sheep is the first clone of an adult animal.
- Chinese leader Deng Xiaoping dies.
- The Labour party wins a landslide victory and Tony Blair becomes Prime Minister.
- A compensation fund for holocaust victims is set up in Switzerland.
- US space shuttle Atlantis docks with the Russian Mir space station.
- Diana, Princess of Wales dies in a car crash in Paris.
- Forest fires in Indonesia cause widespread devastation.
- New Chinese President Tiang visits the USA.
- Hong Kong returns to Chinese rule.
- Over 125 countries sign a treaty banning landmines.
- Mother Teresa of Calcutta dies.

Sporting Life
- Golfer Tiger Woods, 21, becomes the youngest ever winner of the US Masters.
- The Grand National, postponed by a bomb scare, is won by Lord Gyllene.

The Arts
- Titanic' wins the Oscar for best picture
- Arundhati Roy's 'The God of Small Things' wins the 29th Booker Prize
- 'A Taste of Cherry' by Iranian director Abbas Kiarostami won the Cannes ~ilm Festival's Palme d'Or.
- Elton John's re-write of 'Candle in the Wind' in honour of Princess Diana sells over 35 million copies, with profits going to her charities.

1998

World Events of 1998
- President Clinton refuses to resign over the Monika Lewinski scandal.
- A multi-party peace agreement is signed in Northern Ireland
- Economic recession hits Japan.
- The Real IRA who oppose the Good Friday agreement plant a bomb in Omagh, committing the worst atrocity in 30 years of troubles.
- Pol Pot, Cambodian leader responsible for the "Killing Fields" dies.
- India and Pakistan conduct nuclear tests.
- Water is discovered on the moon.
- Spain requests the extradition of ex-Chilean dictator General Pinochet, in hospital in London.
- US astronaut John Glenn, 77, who orbited the earth in 1962, goes into space to assist research into ageing.
- Scientists will not be allowed to clone humans.

Sporting Life
- France beat Brazil to win the World Cup.
- The International Amateur Athletic Federation names Ethiopian, Haile Gebrselassie, athlete of the year.
- Drug scandals overshadow the Tour de France. It is won by Marco Pantani - the first Italian to win for 33 years.

The Arts
- Steven Spielberg's 'Saving Private Ryan' is one of the year's best films,
- Shortly before his death, Ted Hughes publishes 'Birthday Letters', poems about his marriage to the ill-fated Sylvia Plath.
- The Poriuguese writer José Saramago wins the Nobel Prize for Literature.

1999

World Events of 1999
- The race is on to make the world's computer systems Y2K compliant before the end of the year.
- President Clinton survives the attempt to impeach him over the Monica Lewinsy scandal.
- A violent wave of attacks against Christians occurs in Pakistan.
- The health of President Yeltsin and Russian finances are a major cause for concern.
- King Hussein of Jordan dies.
- NATO launches an air attack on Serbia in an attempt to resolve the crisis in Kosovo.
- The Serbian leader, Slobodan Milosevic, could face trial for war crimes in Kosovo.

- Kurdish rebel leader Abdullah Ocalan is arrested by Turkish security forces In Nairobi and later sentenced to death.
- Genetically Modified crops are at the root of the latest food scare.
- The murder of popular British TV presenter, Jill Dando, baffles police and shocks the nation.
- Nuclear powers India and Pakistan confront one another over Kashmir.
- Bertrand Piccard and Brian Jones complete the first non-stop circumnavigation of the globe in a hot air balloon.

Sporting Life
- In American basketball, Michael Jordan of the Chicago Bulls retires.

- The use of performance enhancing drugs is found to be widespread in all sports.
- Manchester United win the English Premier League, the FA Cup and the European Champion's League Cup.

The Arts
- Artefacts from Egyptian Pharoah's tombs go on show in Paris.
- "The Phantom Menace," a new Star Wars movie starring Ewan MacGregor is released.
- Russia marks the 200th anniversary of the birth of the poet, Pushkin.
- Salman Rushdie's novel, "The Ground Beneath Her Feet" wins the Booker prize.

Left:
Liberated Kosovan Albanian refugees welcome NATO troops. However there is doubt as to whether the issues facing the Balkan states can ever be resolved.

Photograph acknowledgements

Cover and title page Globe - Erlendur Berg - Superstock
Hulton Getty 5 right; 12 left; 44 left and right
Mirror Syndication International 10; 27; 32; 33; 37 left; 39; 42; 44; 47; 49; 52; 54 right and centre; 55; 56 right; 57; 59; 60 left; 61 left and right; 66; 70 left; 71; 75 top; 76; 77; 78; 80; 81 top and bottom; 82 top and bottom; 84 bottom and inset; 85; 86 centre and right; 87 left and bottom right; 88; 89.
Illustrated London News 6 left; 8 right; 11 top right; 12 right; 13; 15 inset; 16 top; 17 inset; 18 right and inset left; 19; 20 left; 21; 22; 24; 30;